A Tent in Which to Pass a Summer Night

"Men gain more a thousand times by enlarging the boundary of their thoughts than they do by reading books which echo back to them beliefs they already hold."

"AE" (George Russell) in a letter
to the editor of the *Irish Times*, 1917

A Tent in Which to Pass a Summer Night

George Trevelyan
Belle Valerie Gaunt

STILLPOINT PUBLISHING
WALPOLE, NEW HAMPSHIRE
1985

Dedicated to helpers, visible and invisible,
in grateful acknowledgment of their close co-operation
in the creation of this book.

Acknowledgments

For permission to use copyright material the authors gratefully make the following acknowledgments:

Chapters i - v (Belle Valerie Gaunt):
To Cambridge University Press, from *The Mysterious Universe*, by Sir James Jeans; to Mrs Doris Howe, from *The Mind of the Druid* by Dr. G. Howe; to Sheldon Press, from *The Garden of the Beloved* by Robert Way and *The Wisdom of the Desert* by Thomas Merton; to Chatto and Windus Ltd, from *The Savage and Beautiful Country* by Alan McGlashan; to Wildwood House Ltd, from *Frontiers of Science and Medicine* ed. by Rick J. Carlson; to Oxford University Press, from *January* by R. Bridges and two quotations by Christopher Fry; to Watkins Publishing House, from *Cutting through Spiritual Materialism* by Chogyam Trungpa; to Turnstone Books, from *Jonathan Livingston Seagull* by Richard Bach; to Rudolf Steiner Press, from *The Apocalypse of Saint John* by Rudolf Steiner; to Shanti Sadan, from *Meditation: Its Theory and Practice* by Shastri; to William Collins'Sons & Co. Ltd, from *The Divine Flame*, by Sir A. Hardy, and *The Florentine Renaissance*, by Vincent Cronin; to The Hogarth Press Ltd, from *Jung and the Story of our Time*, by L. van der Post; to Jonathan Cape Ltd, from *Trial by Existence*, by R. Frost; to Neville Spearman, from *Post Mortem Journal* by Jane Sherwood; to Hodder and Stoughton Ltd, from *Her-Bak*, by I.S. de Lubicz, and *The Light and the Gate*, by R. Johnson; to The Compton Press Ltd, from *The Seed of Wisdom*, by J. Hopkins; to William Heinemann Ltd, from *The Song of a Man who has Come Through*, by D.H. Lawrence, and from *Zen and the Art of Motor Cycle Maintenance* by Robert M.

Acknowledgments

Pirsig; to Mr W.N. Perry, from *Treasury of Traditional Wisdom*; to McBride and Broadley — (Agents for New Directions Publications Corporation U.S.A.), for an extract from Arthur Miller's foreword to *The Mind of the Druid*; to Hutchinson Publishing Group Ltd, from *The Occult Way* by P.G. Bowan; to Editions Gallimard, from *Le Petit Prince* by Antoine de Saint-Exupéry; to the Krishnamurti Foundation Trust Ltd, from *You are the World*; to Penguin Books Ltd, from *The Bhagavad Gita* transl. by Juan Mascaró.

Chapter vi (Sir George Trevelyan):
To Clarendon Press Ltd., Oxford, from *Bodily Extension*, by J.C. Earle, and from *A Sleep of Prisoners*, by Christopher Fry; to MacMillan & Co. Ltd., from *Sailing to Byzantium*, by W.B. Yeats; to Faber & Faber Ltd., from *East Coker*, by T.S. Eliot, from *I think Continually* ..., by Stephen Spender, and from *Transfiguration*, by Edwin Muir; to Allen & Unwin Ltd., from *Towards Democracy*, by Edward Carpenter; to Oxford University Press, from *Not in my life time the love envisage...*, by David Gascoyne; to Mrs. George Griffiths, for the poem *Nexus*, by her husband; to The Masefield Trustees (The Society of Authors), for a sonnet by John Masefield.

In a work of this nature, necessarily dependent upon material derived from numerous sources, it is often difficult to ascertain whether or not particular information is in copyright. If we have unwittingly infringed copyright in any way, we tender our sincere apologies and will be glad of the opportunity, upon being satisfied as to the owner's title, to make appropriate acknowledgement in future editions.

Contents

Belle Valerie Gaunt is the author of Chapters I to V; George Trevelyan, of Chapter VI.

Preface

Poetry has a very special function in the spiritual awakening of our time. We are told that the analyzing intellect operates from the left hemisphere of the brain and that in the right hemisphere are located the organs of subtler perception, the artistic and more feminine faculties which can directly apprehend the living Oneness of spirit.

The result of our society's reliance on the masculine faculties of the analyzing intellect has been the atrophying of these organs of subtler perception. They have gone dormant over the last centuries and, as a result, the spiritual worlds have simply disappeared for us. Thus, poetry has too often dropped out or become a merely academic study.

It is of urgent importance for the emergence of a new humanity that the real balance of the intellectual and intuitive faculties should be re-established, and for this, poetry, rightly used, can be a powerful instrument. The quotations in this book have a crystalline quality which can be used to awaken vision and true Imagination.

Preface

Belle Valerie Gaunt has now left us for the higher planes, but I am most certain that she watches with pleasure to see that *A Tent in Which to Pass A Summer Night* will now reach the American public.

Sir George Trevelyan
Gloucestershire, 1985

The Search for Truth

On a huge hill,
Cragged and steep, Truth stands, and he that will
Reach her, about must, and about must go.

John Donne

This stark statement by John Donne vividly depicts the tireless efforts of the weary climber as he ascends the "huge hill, cragged and steep". It also suggests the many sides of truth which are revealed to the aspirant as he wends his way upwards and "about and about". Donne's lines call to mind a story told by Paul Tournier, the Swiss psychologist, of a journey he made from northern Italy back to his native country. Travelling with a fellow countryman, Tournier recounts how, waiting for a train at an Italian wayside station, his friend called his attention to a large poster of the Matterhorn. The artist was incompetent, Tournier's companion declared, having portrayed the silhouette of the mountain inaccurately; the Zmutt ridge had been drawn on the left, whereas everyone knows it was on the right. He had seen it, so he knew. We are left to guess how Tournier gently pointed out that the artist had been looking at the mountain from the Italian side, not from the Swiss. This simple story might well resolve many a heated dispute, demonstrating with visual clarity, as it does, that opposing views may be equally true.

Our preconceived ideas of the truth are often so firm and immovable that we fail to recognise truth when it appears in unexpected guise. Robert Pirsig, in *Zen and the Art of Motorcycle Maintenance*, states the problem thus: "One day Truth knocks on the door, and you say 'Go away, I'm looking for Truth', and so it goes away. Puzzling." André Gide reminds us opportunely that the search for Truth must never be confused with the need for certitudes. And Teilhard de Chardin, one of the greatest prophets of our time, declares that it is the most unexpected that we should come to expect. Conditioned by long years of discipline in the spiritual life, Teilhard was nevertheless courageous enough to be 'open' to direct experience. For this he suffered banishment from his country and a ban on the publication of his books during his lifetime.

Generalisations are proverbially unreliable or untrue. Nevertheless, it might be relevant, in our survey of man's search for Truth, to consider certain points of comparison between the climate of thought which obtained during the Italian Renaissance and that of our own rapidly changing society. In both instances, we see powerful forces at work to discredit, if not muzzle, those whose pioneering spirit and original thought threaten the validity of established authority. In Renaissance Italy, the Church was acknowledged custodian of Truth and constituted the seat of authority. It pronounced definitive judgments on issues of Truth and heresy, and these judgments were not always confined to spiritual affairs. In contemporary society, there exists a similar virtually unquestioned authority — Science. Today, Science sits in judgment on Truth and falsehood. Science provides a generally accepted yardstick by which Truth is measured, accepted or repudiated.

It is true, of course, that at any period in history, certain men of independent minds will arise, whose insatiable curiosity and courage to follow their intuitive powers will lead them beyond the bounds of orthodoxy. In both the Italian Renaissance and the world of today, we can point to examples — men who braved the censure of contemporary authority, daring to incur banishment, death or, more recently, derision and scorn. If we consider the fortunes of three pioneers in throught during the Renaissance, we shall see into what conflicts their unorthodoxy led them, as well as the strength of the forces which opposed their extension of accepted knowledge.

Theophrastus Bombastus von Hohenheim, the great Paracelsus (1490-1541), when appointed physician at Basel in 1526, prefaced his lectures (delivered in German, incidentally, rather than official Latin) by a solemn burning of books. Discrediting past and contemporary medicine, he then proceded to promulgate his own vision. He was, fundamentally, a Hermetic visionary who regarded the life of man as inseparable from that of the cosmos, and contended that a physician must be conversant with a broad spectrum of knowledge, including alchemy and astrology. "Truth is within you," the rebellious physician declares in the oft-quoted poem, 'Paracelsus' by Robert Browning. In the course of his restless life, this controversial and quarrelsome figure struck many a blow for independence of mind, as well as for the courage to accept inspiration and direct knowledge. Eventually, his teachings and his courage cost him his life. But evidence that the flame he helped light still burns today can be seen in such recent publications as *The Frontiers of Science and Medicine*, to which we will return later.

A second Renaissance pioneer is the tragic figure of Galileo, who, after looking through his telescope in 1550, declared that the earth circled the sun and not vice-versa. This scientific discovery had no bearing on religious dogma, nor was it directed against the authority of the Church. Nevertheless, the Church intervened, and Galileo, threatened with torture by the Inquisition, was made to recant. The story is too well known to need elaboration, but it provides one more instance of authority stifling the emergence of new knowledge and seeking to control the frontiers of learning.

A third example is Giordano Bruno, the Dominican monk, born in Naples in 1548 and burnt at the stake for heresy in 1600. Some of Bruno's views have a curiously modern ring, for one of the counts on which the Inquisition condemned him was his belief in the existence of many worlds. Another was his rejection of Ptolemaic astronomy for that of Copernicus. Inspired by Hermetic Neo-Platonists, and especially by Nicholas of Cusa, Bruno asserted that there was something which imparted coherence and intelligibility to all the varying phenomena of the universe. This something, he stated, was God, the universal, unifying substance from which all things issue. After seven years of solitary imprisonment in Rome, Bruno remained steadfast in his refusal to recant. He was burnt to death in the Campo di Fiore, where a bronze statue has been erected to his memory.

Today, those who come forward with teachings unacceptable to established Science may suffer scorn and derision from that stronghold of authority.

Compared to pioneers of three or four centuries ago, however, they have less to fear. The Church was more ruthless in its suppression of new truths than are the scientific pundits of today — however much the latter may dislike having their theories and 'laws' disturbed.

There is no doubt that we are living at a time of breakthrough. Since the discovery of energy fields, horizons of the knowable are being rapidly extended, and the very nature of man himself is recognised as far more complex and mysterious than was supposed a century ago. It is not without reason that Alexis Carrel entitles his book *L'homme, cet inconnu*. The words of Earl Balfour, uttered shortly after the turn of the century, seem to me of such profound importance that they deserve pride of place in the choice of quotations that follows. Indeed, their implications will never be far from my mind throughout the subsequent pages:

Our highest truths are but half-truths;
Think not to settle down for ever in any truth.
Make use of it as a tent in which to pass a summer's night,
But build no house of it, or it will be your tomb.
When you first have an inkling of its insufficiency
And begin to descry a dim counter-truth looming up beyond,
Then weep not, but give thanks:
It is the Lord's voice whispering,
'Take up thy bed and walk'.

The Search for Truth

In glancing back over the centuries, we can become disenchanted with the effects of dogmatic teaching and rebellious in the face of authority, especially when our personal beliefs are at stake. But what lessons can we learn from the past? How should we proceed to learn them? How, indeed, should we direct our thought and attention? Krishnamurti suggests a line of approach with the theme of Direct Experience which runs through so much of his writings and teachings, and more and more modern spokesmen are suggesting that "truth is within us" and that knowledge is experience, not a formula. The surge of interest in meditation during the last few years bears witness to the growing numbers who are attempting the "journey inwards", seeking self-knowledge and direct experience. Teachers from both East and West are encouraging the true seeker to look within to discover his own true nature and his relationship to "the Source" — his relationship to what we call God.

> In truth, we seek for God outside of ourselves until we make the great discovery, which is that our heart is the sanctuary where the Lord of the universe dwells in all his glory.
>
> *Swami Ramdas*

Across the centuries, we find the same principle anticipated by Saint Augustine:

7

I found Thee not, O Lord, without, because I
erred in seeking Thee without, that wert within.

Another gleam of light comes to us not only from a
distant pre-Christian era, but from a culture and
tradition quite different from our own. We find it in
The Upanishads:

That God, the all-worker, the Great self
Ever seated in the heart of creatures
Is framed by the heart, by the thought, by the mind;
They who know that become immortal.

Saint Augustine, again, tells us that:

It is with the interior eye that truth is seen.

And in the *Hermetica,* we find the following statement:

The things that are in the spiritual world can be
seen by the eye of the mind alone.

For those interested in the theory and practise of
meditation, there is a useful little book by an Indian
sage, Hari Prasad Shastri, a student of the holy classics
of ancient India and China for over forty years. It is
worth noting what Shastri says about meditation:

Meditation brings into action the faculty of intuition (*buddhi*) and it is this mystical sense which gives us the capacity to approach the absolute Truth. Hume maintains that Truth is inaccessible and unapproachable but this is not so. The Sufis and the Indian and Jewish mystics all declare that Truth is knowable and teach this way of approach. The faculty which can apprehend truth is not special to a privileged few; it is latent in all, in the sinner and in the saint.

By cultivating intuition, we can meditate on God, but to do so we must leave the discursive reason on one side for the time being. In order to *know* God, even intuition is not enough; there is yet another faculty to be aroused — that of vision. Unless we *see* God, we shall not know Him, and the spirit of man *can* see God. The word 'see' is perhaps not the right one, but it appears to be the best we can use. We *see;* we *know;* we *realise;* this is absolute knowledge, direct experience, whereby God becomes real to us, and in us.

When we use the words 'to see' as synonymous with 'to know', we find ourselves in the company of many seekers after Truth, each of whom may help to broaden our understanding and deepen our vision. One such is Hermes Trismegistus, that great teacher of ancient Egyptian wisdom who is pictured in the marble paving near the west door of Siena Cathedral, handing on the ancient wisdom to Moses. In one passage, he speaks as follows:

> Let us all with one accord give praise to Him, who is seated high upon the heavens, creator of all that is. It is He who is the eye of my mind.

Among the wealth of other testimony, we might consider the following:

> The eye by which I see God is the same as the eye by which God sees us.
>
> *Meister Eckhart*

> Our whole business, therefore, in this life is to restore to health the eye of the heart whereby God may be seen.
>
> *Saint Augustine*

> On ne voit bien qu'avec le coeur.
>
> *Saint Exupéry*

As Hermes himself states:

> Languages differ, my son, but mankind is one; and speech likewise is one. It is translated from tongue to tongue, and we find it to be the same in

Egypt, Persia or Greece ... Speech, then, is an image of intellect; and intellect is an image of God.

Or, as *The Golden Tract* sums up:

> Such men there have been in all countries. Amongst the Egyptians, Hermes Trismegistus holds the highest place; then come Chaldeans, Greeks, Arabs, Italians, Gauls, Englishmen, Dutchmen, Spaniards, Germans, Poles, Hungarians, Hebrews and many others. Though the aforementioned sages wrote at different times, and in different languages, yet their works exhibit so marvellous an agreement.

Marsilio Ficino, a Florentine student of Greek born in 1433, was commissioned by Cosimo I to translate into Latin the works of both Hermes and Plato. He could not have made a more apt choice, for Ficino, as Vincent Cronin tells us in *The Florentine Renaissance;*

> ... had a tendency to visions, and ... Plato would seem to appear to him ... One of the phenomena which most interested him, and which he himself experienced, was 'vacatio mentis', when the soul frees itself from the body.

11

More recent investigation has established credence for 'out of the body' experiences; and such texts as those written through the agency of Geraldine Cummings (cited in Raynor Johnson's *The Light and the Gate*) provides evidence for the influence of disincarnate beings on living writers. On the basis of such evidence, it is possible that Ficino's translations of Plato were not entirely unaided, but involved a blending of two worlds. As Cronin tells us, Ficino, between 1459 and 1477, translated the complete works of the Greek philosopher,

> ... and was thus the first man for many centuries to discover the historical Plato. It was an exciting discovery, a philosophic America. Ficino found himself confronted with a closely argued theocentric system of great power and beauty, attaching the highest importance to love of God and one's neighbour — yet written 350 years before Christ. Ficino's reaction was to treat it not as a stumbling-block to the faith but as a precursory work comparable to the Old Testament — Plato he called a 'Moses speaking Attic Greek'. He set out to harmonise Plato's thought and Christianity in a system of his own.

Perhaps we should permit Ficino to describe how he did so in his own words:

12

There are some persons, though very few such are to be found, who burn with eagerness to attain truth; but they do not have faith that it can be investigated through its human traces, in which the ambiguous minds of most natural philosophers are accustomed to trust. Therefore they give themselves to God and don't attempt anything by themselves. With open and purified eyes, they wait for what may be shown by God, and this is what Socrates is said to have taught and to have done.

More than 2000 years later, Sir James Jeans has this to say:

Our difficulties have all arisen from an initial assumption that everything in Nature, and waves of light in particular, admitted of a mechanical explanation: we tried in brief to treat the universe as a large machine ... If the universe is a universe of thought, then its creation must have been an act of thought. Indeed, the finiteness of time and space almost compel us, of themselves, to picture the creation as an act of thought.

And this, as well:

Time and space, which form the setting for the thought, must have come into being as part of this act. Primitive cosmologies pictured a Creator working in space and time, forging sun, moon and stars out of already existent raw material. Modern scientific theory compels us to think of the Creator as working outside time and space, which are part of his creation, just as the artist is outside his canvas. 'Non in tempore, sed cum tempore, finxit Deus mundum.' Indeed, the doctrine dates back as far as Plato.

Which brings us full circle, for as Plato himself says:

> Time and the heavens came into being at the same instant, in order that, if they were ever to dissolve, they might be dissolved together. Such was the mind and thought of God in the creation of time.

Joseph Roux speaks of the faculties of intuition and presentiment often developed and employed by creative artists:

> That which we know is but little: that which we have a presentiment of is immense. It is in this direction that the poet outruns the learned man.

George Russell, the Irish mystic poet who wrote under the pseudonyn of A.E., speaks with first-hand authority on the intuitive faculty:

> I start in deepest reverence with God in whom I believe intuitively — not for any reasons advanced by the mind. In contemplating the Supreme Being, it is most fitting to be silent, aware that while the human mind is an instrument of value in its proper sphere, it is wholly incapable of grasping the highest reality — the quality of consciousness which we call Spirit. If we feel driven to philosophise, we can do no other than take the highest values we know: Love, Truth, Beauty, Wisdom, etc., and regard the Supreme Being as the Source and Sustainer of these values. We may think of God, the Creator, as least imperfectly described as Divine Imagining.

The theme of 'Divine Imagining' has been developed, in a strikingly interesting way, by Raynor Johnson in his book, *Nurslings of Immortality*. The circumstances and events which inspired this work are vividly presented in another of Johnson's books, *The Light and the Gate*. This deserves more attention, and we shall return to it in Chapter V. For the moment, it will be worth our while to consider some of Shastri's teaching, which clarifies and supplements much of what we have been discussing:

15

The spirit of man is God in a conditioned form. It is only this element in man, his real Self (Atman), which can know God.

When this knowledge of God, or Self-realisation, comes, then there follows that spiritual peace which is called *Shanti* in Sanscript and *Salem* by Jews. Those who have acquired the realisation of this spiritual peace can bear witness to the Truth, calm and undaunted, even under a shower of bullets. If their dearest friend betrays them, they are like a great mountain, immovable in the midst of storm, with its highest peak lit by the dazzling sunlight.

We are here in the world to realise this perfect peace and freedom, and when it is attained, life becomes worthwhile. Then the bird's song finds an echo in our hearts, and all the loveliness of nature is a reflection of that which is within our souls. Meditation is one of the ways by which this peace and joy is to be obtained.

It is written: "Without *knowledge* there is no salvation", not, "Without *meditation* there is no salvation". Meditation *per se* is valueless. It is merely the method whereby the knowledge of God-realisation is attained, and herein lies its real value. Meditation itself is a technique for purifying the psychological instruments of knowledge, and for awakening their faculty of spiritual intuition.

Mind is a great creative force, and its

16

creativeness comes into operation in a condition of perfect silence. Accumulation of energy leads to creation. When we sit in meditation, we stop our senses from functioning, and an accumulation of mental energy is stored up in the psychic region. Invisible forces come into play, inspiration wells up and the imagination becomes refined in its function. The mind when stilled becomes creative, but in order to create spiritual forms of everlasting beauty, like Dante's epic, Kalidasa's *Shakuntala* or the spiritual peace (*Shanti*) of Yoga, it must also be illumined. The mind imbibes the quality of its experience: it is, in a sense, like a wax tablet on which past impressions are recorded. It thus receives impressions, not only through the senses but also from the store of past thoughts and feelings, which emerge under the incentive of kindred association. This store is the seat of memory and imagination, and it is continually being replenished. Our present character is thus very much influenced by our past thoughts, and it is essential to realise that what we interest ourselves in and feel strongly about at the present time, sinks into the substance of the mind and will return to us intensified in the future. We must, therefore, be discriminating in the matter of our thoughts...

The mind is like a bird pecking in a field, always pecking at and picking up something; what is important is that is should select wisely. All that the senses report is woven into something which tends either to destroy or to build up the mind, for the mind assimilates that upon which it dwells. If it broods on crime, then it will become filled with a store of that quality of thought.

Yoga does not believe in killing any part of our psychological instrument: its aim is to train, to transform, and use it in the right way. It is clear that we cannot live the best life unless our mind is tranquillised, for only then does it receive the divine light from its original source within the personality. Hatred and fanaticism introduce qualities which coarsen the mind, impairing mental health; but selfless thoughts are pure, for they seek the well-being of all and unite the puny individual mind with the Cosmic Mind, the mind of God, which rules alike the stars in their courses, the electrons in their orbits, and governs the emergence of the infinitely varied forms of life.

Meditation means, amongst other things, the tranquillisation and purification of the mind. The ground must be prepared for this by the expulsion from the mind of all that is mean and degrading, all that does not promote the well-being of society and the individual. All thoughts of duality and separation, and also all desires which impede spiritual

18

progress must be carefully eliminated, and harboured no more.

A good illustration of the necessity of emptying the mind of its contents is given in a Zen story. There was in Japan a Zen monk who was an adept in meditation. Among the men from all walks of life who were attracted by his reputation as a teacher was a well-known professor of the Imperial University of Tokyo. The professor went to see the monk, who offered him the customary green tea. Placing a cup before the distinquished visitor, he poured the tea into it until it became full. He continued to pour, and the cup overflowed. Seeing the tea spilling over the table and on to the floor mats, the startled professor asked for an explanation. The Zen monk said: "I can fill what is empty, but not what is already full. You have come to me with your mind full of ideas of *meum* and *tuum*, ambitions and desires. If you seek my instruction, empty your mind, forget all you have learned, and rid yourself of all harmful and useless matter; then return, and I will teach you."

The texture of the mind is coarsened and rendered opaque by narrowness, prejudice, and all selfishness and accentuation of egoity. The mind must be made light throughout all its layers, that is, throughout the instinctive, emotional, intuitional and spiritual planes. This is done by admitting into it only the purest thoughts, and by practising meditation and

19

contemplation so that the quietened mind may offer no impediment to the divine flow. When the mind is ruled in this way, it becomes a boon to ourselves and others.

It is said that there are as many ways and methods of meditation as there are people wishing to learn and practise it. In all of them, the objective is the same. Surely what is most essential is the attempt to purify our instruments, to clean the windows of our souls. Only then may light stream in unimpeded; only then may we eventually become aware of our potential divinity and attain a closer and more conscious union with 'our source', the Creator, the Heavenly Father, Divine Beneficence, or whatever name we employ. Our search for truth will only become fruitful if it is shot through with a broad tolerance and deep understanding. As George Santayana states:

I do not ask anyone to think in my terms, if he prefers others. Let him clean better, if he can, the windows of his soul, that the variety and beauty of the prospect may spread more brightly before him.

II

Choice and Free Will

The enquiring mind engaged in the unremitting
search for truth is invariably assailed, as Wordsworth
says, by.

> obstinate questionings
> Of sense and outward things,
> Black misgivings of a creature
> Moving about in worlds not realised.

We all recognise this state of mind. The 'obstinate
questionings' inevitably lead to a single central
problem — is there a meaning and purpose in life, and
what is our part in it? Confronted by apparent
injustice, inequality and suffering, by evil and hatred,
many are driven to deny the existence of an all-
powerful, all-wise and all-loving Creator. How, one
may ask, can a benevolent Creator allow the horrifying
abuses that exist all around us? If one short life on

21

earth is all we can expect, it no longer seems to make sense.

To the Western mind, conditioned by Western values and Western culture, it may come as a surprise to learn that *more than half the population of the world accepts the basic teaching of reincarnation and karma as fundamental to its religious belief.* It may also be surprising that, in the early Christian Church, reincarnation as a doctrine was not declared heretical until 545 AD.

Now, at the dawn of a new age, more and more individuals in the West are discovering meaning in Eastern thought and in the teachings of ancient wisdom. And in the edifice of world philosophies, reincarnation and Karma stand as perhaps the two great central pillars. Through an appreciation of these central pillars, we can learn a new exhilaration, springing from the realisation that life does indeed have a purpose, that a great plan does indeed exist, devised and governed by what Grahame Howe calls 'Infinite Benevolence'. Through appreciation of these central pillars, we can begin to realise that we live our lives — many lifetimes — according to a pattern of free-will, subject to spiritual laws.

What are these laws, and how can we bring ourselves into accord with them? Karma, the law of cause and effect, is implicit in much Christian teaching — 'As a man sows, so shall he reap', for example — and is sometimes imperfectly understood when described as Eastern fatalism. Another and related law is that 'like attracts like'. The implications of these laws are more far-reaching and profound than may at first be apparent. We shall return to those implications in Part V.

Much spiritual teaching accepts the premise that man is a being of soul or spirit, who inhabits a physical body which he discards at the end of each earth life — rather as a butterfly discards the chrysalis shell for which it has no further use. Given this premise, each earth life becomes an opportunity for learning lessons and making spiritual progress; and the wisdom and knowledge assimilated in one earth life is carried forwards into the next, where it becomes available as intuition. Thus, man lives his successive lives on this planet (and possibly on others as well) in a dense physical body of low vibration, the vehicle of the self or soul-spirit. Between incarnations, he returns to another sphere (invisible only because of its much more rapid vibrations) and there, in what is largely a 'thought world', he learns and grows in understanding. Finally, when the time is ripe, he chooses, of his own free will, to reincarnate, and he even chooses the circumstances of the life into which he will be born. Before entering that life, he sees a 'blue-print' of it, so to speak; but at birth he forgets the choice he has made. As Robert Frost states in his poem, 'Trial by

23

Choice and Free Will

Existence': "The pure fate to which you go / Admits no memory of the choice." This poem requires careful study and profound thought, which may well transform many of the reader's attitudes. For once one becomes aware of one's choice, and of having made it, one cannot harbour a sense of injustice or unfairness.

From 'Trial by Existence'

And from a cliff-top is proclaimed
    The gathering of the souls for birth,
The trial by existence named,
    The obscuration upon earth.
And the slant spirits trooping by
    In streams and cross- and counter-streams
Can but give ear to that sweet cry
    For its suggestion of what dreams!

And the more loitering are turned
    To view once more the sacrifice
Of those who for some good discerned
    Will gladly give up paradise.
And a white shimmering concourse rolls
    Toward the throne to witness there
The speeding of devoted souls
    Which God makes his especial care.

24

Choice and Free Will

And none are taken but who will,
    Having first heard the life read out
That opens earthward, good and ill,
    Beyond the shadow of a doubt;
And very beautifully God limns,
    And tenderly, life's little dream,
But naught extenuates or dims,
    Setting the thing that is supreme.

Nor is there wanting in the press
    Some spirit to stand simply forth,
Heroic in its nakedness,
    Against the uttermost of earth.
The tale of earth's unhonoured things
    Sounds nobler there than 'neath the sun;
And the mind whirls and the heart sings,
    And a shout greets the daring one.

But always God speaks at the end:
    'One thought in agony of strife
The bravest would have by for friend,
    The memory that he chose the life;
But the pure fate to which you go
    Admits no memory of choice,
Or the woe were not earthly woe
    To which you gave the assenting voice.'

Choice and Free Will

And so the choice must be again,
   But the last choice is still the same;
And the awe passes wonder then,
   And a hush falls for all acclaim.
And God has taken a flower of gold
   And broken it, and used therefrom
The mystic link to bind and hold
   Spirit to matter till death come.

'Tis of the essence of life here,
   Though we choose greatly, still to lack
The lasting memory at all clear,
   That life has for us on the rack
Nothing but what we somehow chose;
   Thus are we wholly stripped of pride
In the pain that has but one close,
   Bearing it crushed and mystified.

It is not only interesting but also significant that the basic vision expressed in this work recurs in that of other poets. I mention but one. Kathleen Raine, in 'Lachesis', skillfully draws together many strands of thought separated by long centuries, thus weaving a tapestry arresting in its appeal.

26

Choice and Free Will

The poet introduces strands of imaginative thought from Plotinus, Blake, Plato, and later from the ancient Veda and The Book of the Dead. The possibility that we have chosen the life in which we now find ourselves immersed is certainly suggested. I would be inclined to clarify this with contemporary esoteric teaching that we are indeed permitted to choose the circumstances of that life before incarnation, yet freewill as to how we act within those circumstances is always retained. We are left by Kathleen Raine to find our way through a maze of suggested ideas, and are only led towards the light of some reassurance by the words of Mother Julian of Norwich: "All shall be well..."

There are many streams of esoteric teaching that corroborate the theme in both this poem and Frost's. For many of us, these teachings have the ring of truth and awaken a response from some hidden repository of accumulated knowledge deep within us. In *The Seed of Wisdom*, John Hopkins, a student of the Arcane School founded in 1923 by Alice Bailey, writes:

When it comes to spiritual progress, we discover two additional factors which carry us along the path that leads unerringly towards the goal. One is the knowledge that we are not alone in our

27

endeavour, and the other is our inherent sense of divinity.

There are of course many roads that we can take towards that distant goal; and in the initial stages of the journey much will depend on what appear to be accidental circumstances; such as where we were born, and therefore what religion we were taught in our youth; and what sort of family background has influenced our early life, and what inspiration — if any — has ever come our way.

The Ageless Wisdom teaching prompts us to question whether all, or indeed any, of these factors, are as accidental as they at first appear. Once we accept the reality of the soul as the real centre of consciousness in man, and the personality and the physical body as one of the many 'outer garments of the soul', we begin to realise that these apparently accidental features of our lives are, to an increasing extent in the long life of the soul, a deliberate choice. The vision is clear — to the soul — but the trouble is that for countless lives there is no registering of the vision in the brain.

But once the many futile and restless activities of the brain have been stilled, and the emotional nature has been brought somewhat under control, the purpose of the life as visioned by the soul can be sensed. We then discover that all roads lead to the Path of truly conscious spiritual endeavour, which means service to the Plan. And then comes understanding, wisdom, serenity — and much hard work.

III

Acceptance

The meaning behind Frost's poem may evoke a response from the deeper layers of our consciousness and may seem to possess the ring of truth. If it does, our outlook on life may well undergo a radical change. If we realise that, in each successive incarnation, we have chosen the life and circumstances in which we find ourselves, we cannot contend that we are unhappy victims, or complain of our ill-luck, or bewail the unfairness of fate. Instead, we can learn the lessons vital to further progress. As we have already noted, knowledge and wisdom absorbed in one life are carried forward into those that follow, and become available as intuition. Similarly, Karmic 'debts' are carried forward, to be met and paid; and thus the problem of difficult relationships, for example, becomes an opportunity for practising the law of Love. One may even come to see all difficulties as blessings, the best possible opportunities for learning and making progress. A statement by Pascal is particularly pertinent here: "Les événements sont les maîtres que Dieu nous envoie." That eloquent plea for acceptance is a suitable introduction to this chapter.

But the word 'acceptance' evokes reactions of great variety. It may, for example, be taken to imply a weak and passive acquiescence, a lack of courage and enterprise in the face of obstacles. Such a defeatist attitude, however — often accompanied by expressions of powerlessness and denials of responsibility — is directly opposed to the meaning intended here. We will, rather adopt the significance of the word as explained by Dr. Graham Howe in 'The Open Way'. In an introduction to Howe's last book, *The Mind of the Druid*, written in 1975, Henry Miller offers a clarification of 'acceptance':

> The art of living is based on rhythm, on give and take, ebb and flow, light and dark, life and death. By acceptance of all the aspects of life, good and bad, right and wrong, yours and mine, the static defensive life, which is what most people are cursed with, is converted into a dance, 'the dance of life', as Havelock Ellis called it. The real function of the dance is metamorphosis...

In Howe's broad, balanced perspective, death is neither the 'last enemy' nor the 'end'; and if the healer

31

has a role, Howe suggests that 'it is to play the part of gynaecologist to death'. In short:

> There is nothing that it is not better to accept, even though it be the expression of our enemy's ill-will. There is no progress other than what is, if we could let it be...

And, as Henry Miller observes on the above passage:

> This idea of 'let be', of non-interference, of living now in the moment, fully, with complete faith in the process of life, which must remain largely unknown to us, is the cardinal aspect of Howe's philosophy.

Sustained contact with Howe's thought may well transform our own conception of 'acceptance'. It may enlarge our horizons and deepen our understanding. We may eventually come to share his vision of the ultimate triumph of 'Infinite Benevolence' and of the wholeness of life; and, in doing so, we may ourselves become more whole.

Nor is Howe alone in advocating acceptance. It is something that writers through the centuries have encouraged us to cultivate, looking with confidence for the ultimate good in what at first may appear wholly evil. As Shakespeare says:

Acceptance

There is some soul of goodness in things evil,
Would men observingly distill it out;
Thus may we gather honey from the weed.

Robert Bridges treats the same theme in his poem,
'January', the last verse of which repays reading and re-
reading. The profound truth it contains throws light
on many seemingly incomprehensible situations:

'January'

Cold is the winter day, misty and dark:
The sunless sky with faded gleams is rent.
And patches of thin snow outlying, mark
The landscape with a drear disfigurement.

No birds sing, but the starling chaps his bill
And chatters mockingly; the newborn lambs
Within their strawbuilt fold beneath the hill
Answer with plaintive cry their bleating dams.

Their voices melt in welcome dreams of spring,
Green grass and leafy trees and sunny skies:
My fancy decks the woods, the thrushes sing,
Meadows are gay, bees hum and scents arise.

And God the Maker doth my heart grow bold
To praise for wintry works not understood,
Who all the worlds and ages doth behold,
Evil and good as one, and all as good.

Acceptance

Man is constantly making judgments from too limited and restricted a perspective. He is, as it were, 'blinkered', and therefore habitually mistakes a short-term result for the ultimate. We need the eye of the poet to see beyond this restricted vision, as well as a patient and understanding heart to have unwavering faith in 'Infinite Benevolence' and the inevitable *eventual* triumph of the Powers of Light.

One of the stories in *The Garden of the Beloved* by Robert Way illustrates, in a colourful fashion, the eventual emergence of good from apparent evil:

Now the Garden was full of birds with beautiful plumage which sang continually the praise of the Beloved, and of brightly coloured butterflies which played about the flowers so that the bushes seemed to blaze with a splendour not their own.

One day as the Disciple was passing through the Garden, he noticed that the leaves of certain plants were ragged and full of holes. Then looking more closely he saw there were on them many small caterpillars, dung-coloured and covered with hideous hairs, which even as he looked were eating the leaves of the plants.

When he saw this it seemed to him that they were doing great harm to the Garden of the Beloved, so he plucked them one by one from the plants and crushed them beneath his heel.

At that moment, the Lover came through the Garden and when he saw what the Disciple was doing, he wept, yet he spoke gently to the Disciple and said, "I know that you have acted through ignorance and with a good heart in doing this, yet in doing it you have greatly hurt the beauty of the Garden of the Beloved."

The Disciple when he heard this was amazed and very sorrowful.

The Lover then showed the Disciple another plant where he saw the caterpillars enveloping themselves in cocoons of silk. There were many cocoons on the stems of the leaves and even as he watched, one split and from it came a butterfly with wings like the rainbow. Then he perceived in his ignorance he had hurt the Garden of the Beloved.

If one dwells upon a theme of such importance and ponders it for days and weeks, the main stream of thought will be joined by many tributaries, like little streams coming down from the mountains and flowing into a broad river in a valley. Or as iron filings are drawn by a magnet, so creative thought has an energy all its own, which draws other thoughts towards it.

Le Petit Prince by Antoine de Saint-Exupéry is a source of many such tributaries which flow into the main theme of our thought and investigation. As the Petit Prince says to the stranded airman, for example: "Ce qui embellit le desert, c'est qu'il cache un puit quelquepart." The Psalmist of old expresses a similar idea in the well-known words:

> Blessed is the man whose strength is in thee: in whose heart are thy ways. Who going through the vale of misery useth it for a well: and the pools are filled with water.

From an unshakeable faith in the triumph of goodness, acceptance of the whole of life — together with all it brings — can flow freely. Here is an old Chinese parable which I cherish:

> Long years ago there lived in China an old Tao farmer. He possessed one horse which was very dear to him. One day, the horse ran away. Next day, the neighbour came to commiserate with the farmer and offer him his condolence. But the farmer answered him: "Who knows what is good and what is bad?" Next day, the horse returned, bringing with him six wild horses from the hills. Next day the neighbour called to offer his congratulations; but the farmer only replied: "Who knows what is

36

good and what is bad?" Next day his son mounted one of the wild horses, trying to break it in, but was thrown and broke his leg. Next day the neighbour called to commiserate, but the farmer replied: Who knows what is good and what is bad?" On the following day, soldiers called to conscript young men for the army, and asked for the farmer's son. Seeing his broken leg, they departed, leaving him at home with his old father.

And William Blake, with characteristic simplicity, expresses the kernel of our theme in a few immortal lines:

> Joy and woe are woven fine,
> A clothing for the soul divine;
> Under every grief and pine
> Runs a joy with silken twine.

In order to understand and enter into the state of acceptance suggested by these quotations, two things are particularly necessary. First, one must be prepared to take a long-term view. Second, one must have a living conviction of the reality of a plan, whose Author is Divine Beneficence. It is surely from this experience that Mother Julian of Norwich speaks when she says: "And all shall be well / And all manner of things shall be well." And in *Jonathan Livingston Seagull*, Richard

Acceptance

Bach manages to convey to contemporary readers truths so profound and even obscure that, although reiterated by writers for more than two thousand years, they have frequently been unnoticed or ignored. As one example, we may cite a conversation between Jonathan Seagull and his friend, Fletcher, after Jonathan has been attacked by a flock of gulls who despise him for being 'different':

> "Jonathan, remember what you said a long time ago, about loving the flock enough to return to it and help it learn?"
> "Yes."
> "I don't understand how you manage to love a mob of birds that have just tried to kill you."
> "Oh, Fletch, you don't love that! You don't love hatred and evil, of course. You have to practise and see the real gull, the good in every one of them, and to help them see it in themselves. That's what I mean by love. It's fun, when you get the knack of it."

The spirit of acceptance — acceptance of the whole of life as it is — may perhaps bring us nearer to an understanding of one of the most apparently difficult sayings of Jesus:

> Ye have heard that it hath been said, Thou shalt

38

love thy neighbour, and hate thine enemy. But I say unto you, Love your enemies, bless them that curse you, do good to them that hate you, and pray for them that despitefully use you, and persecute you.

In *Cutting through Spiritual Materialism*, Chogyam Trungpa, a contemporary Buddhist monk, illuminates our thought and imagination, enabling us to perceive the connexion between the spirit of acceptance and the seemingly impossible injunction to love our enemies:

In order to develop love — universal love, cosmic love, whatever you would like to call it — one must accept the whole situation of life as it is, both the light and the dark, the good and the bad. One must open oneself to life, communicate with it. Perhaps you are fighting to develop love and peace, struggling to achieve them: "We are going to make it, we are going to spend thousands of dollars in order to broadcast the doctrine of love everywhere, we are going to proclaim love." Okay, proclaim it, do it, spend your money, but what about the speed and aggression behind what you are doing? Why do you have to push us into the acceptance of love? Why is there such speed and force involved? If your love is moving with the same speed and drive as other people's hatred, then something appears to

Acceptance

be wrong. It would seem to be the same as calling darkness light. There is so much ambition involved, taking the form of proselytising.

It is not an open situation of communication with things as they are. The ultimate implication of the words 'peace on earth' is to remove altogether the ideas of peace and war and to open yourself equally and completely to the positive and negative aspects of the world. It is like seeing the world from an aerial point of view: there is light, there is dark; both are accepted.

This 'aerial point of view' encourages and enhances the conception of the oneness of life; and from such extended vision arises a fuller comprehension of acceptance. Birth and death are seen as simply events in one continuous process of life. Long before the Christian era, Plato understood this when he wrote: "The living come from the dead, just as the dead go to the living." And Goethe, contemplating death in his old age, sees it as part of a benevolent process:

The thought of death leaves me in perfect peace, for I have a firm conviction that our spirit is a being of indestructible nature. It works on from eternity to eternity; it is like the sun, which, though it seems to set to our mortal eyes, does not really set, but shines on perpetually.

40

Acceptance

When death is seen as a metamorphosis whereby the soul is released from the limitations of the physical body, it can be welcomed — not so much as a way out of mortal suffering as a birth into a thought-world where conditions of limitless beauty and creativity provide the opportunity for endless progress. In the following poem, Walt Whitman not only accepts death, but, like Goethe, welcomes it with eager expectation:

Come, lovely and soothing death,
Undulate round the world, serenely arriving,
                     arriving,
In the day, in the night, to all, to each,
Sooner or later delicate death.

Praised be the fathomless universe,
For life and joy, and for objects and knowledge
                     curious,
And for love, sweet love — but praise! praise!
                     praise!
For the sure-enwinding arms of cool-enfolding
                     death.

Dark mother always gliding near with soft feet,
Have none enchanted for thee a chant of fullest
                     welcome?
Then I chant if for thee, I glorify thee above all,

Acceptance

I bring thee a song that when thou must indeed
      come, come unfalteringly.

Over the tree-tops I float thee a song,
Over the rising and sinking waves, over the myriad
      fields and the prairies wide,
Over the dense-packed cities all and the teeming
      wharves and waves,
I float this carol with joy, with joy to thee,
      O death.

IV

Knowledge and Wisdom

Between our birth and death we may touch
understanding,
As a moth brushes a window with its wing.

Christopher Fry

With the vision enlarged to include many lives in a
pattern of freewill, and with death no longer the
enemy but a friendly process, we can turn now quite
naturally to the problem of acquiring knowledge and
wisdom on the long journey.

It has been said that just as the body needs food and
air and exercise to maintain health, so the soul needs
experience. Keats spoke of the world as "the Vale of
soul-making". Experience is the food of the soul, and
when this is digested, what is assimilated is retained
as wisdom. Moreover, wisdom absorbed in one lifetime
is carried forward to the next, when it becomes
available as intuition. Such teaching underlines the

43

importance of not interfering with the law of cause and effect, for example, of not trying to stand between our children or friends and the results of their actions. With the most well-meaning of parents and teachers, this often seems difficult. In *The Occult Way*, P.G. Bowen puts the case for personal experience:

> Better far to err through ignorance than do right blindly at the direction of another. For in one case the man learns from his mistakes and so profits; in the other the man learns nothing at all and suffers in one degree or another through abandonment of individual responsibility.

Knowledge is experience, not a formula. This theme is treated by many writers, but few insist on it with a more passionate appeal than Krishnamurti. Although his thought and exposition may at first seem difficult or obscure, they repay patient study and practise. The following quotation is from a book entitled *You Are the World*, a collection of his talks at universities:

> Our minds are conditioned by formulas: my experience, my knowledge, my family, my country, like and dislike, hate, jealousy, envy, sorrow, the fear of this and the fear of that. That is the circle, the wall behind which I live. And I am not only afraid of what is within, but even more so of what is

beyond the wall. One can observe this fact very simply in oneself without having to read a great many books, study philosophy and all the rest of it. It may very well be that because one reads so much what others have said that one knows nothing about oneself, what one actually is, and what is actually taking place in oneself. If we looked in ourselves, ignoring what we think we should be seen but seeing what we actually are, then, perhaps, we would discover for ourselves the existence of these formulas and concepts — which are really prejudices and bias — that divide man against man. And so, in all relationships between man and man, there is fear and conflict — not only the conflict of sexual rights, of territorial rights, but also the conflict between what has been, is and what should be.

When one observes this fact in oneself — not as an idea, not as something that you look in at from outside the window — but actually see in yourself, then one can find out whether it is at all possible to uncondition the mind of all formulas, of all beliefs, prejudices and fears and thereby, perhaps, live at peace. We see that man, both historically and in present times, has accepted war as a way of life. So to end war — not any particular war but all wars — how to live utterly at peace without any conflict becomes a question not only for the intellect, but one that must be answered *totally*, not fragmentarily or in specialised fields. Can man — you and I — live completely at peace — which doesn't mean living a dull life, or one that has no active, driving energy — can we find out if such a peace is possible? Surely it must be possible, otherwise our life has very little meaning....

So, presuming that one is sufficiently serious, what is our problem? How to live our daily life here — not in a monastary or some romantic dream world, not in some emotional, dogmatic, drug-ridden world — but here and now, every day; how to live at great peace, with great intelligence, without any frustration or fear, to live so completely, so in a state of bliss — which, of course, implies meditation — that, really, is the basic problem. And also whether it is possible to understand this whole life, not in fragments, but completely: be completely involved in it, and not committed to any part of it; to be involved with the total process of living without any conflict, misery, confusion or sorrow. That is the real question. For only then can one bring about a different world. That is the *real* revolution, the inward psychological revolution from which springs an immediate outward revolution. Let us, then, take the journey together — and I mean together, not you sitting there and I sitting on the platform — to look together at this whole field of life so that we understand it; not for someone else to understand it and then tell us to understand it. Then only will we be both teacher and disciple.

Explicit in this thought-provoking passage is an invitation to direct experience, and it is clear that Krishnamurti is talking about that which is familiar to him. One can discern a similar first-hand knowledge in the words of Dr. Graham Howe:

> Once you have come to depend on text books and structured ideas about complexes and diagnoses, you have got yourself into a world of phantasy which can only stand between you and the object of your experience, which is the patient who has just come into your consulting room.

Howe goes on to make this impressive statement:

> When it comes to the *religion of experience*, I certainly claim that I believe in Infinite Benevolence. I believe that the Infinite Benevolence created the world and everything in the world from the stars to the fishes and the flies, including every one of us; and I believe that we are all interdependent, balanced in this ecology of the great experience of living.

Knowledge and Wisdom

Here is a fearless statement of personal belief which makes no attempt to conform to any official creed or orthodoxy, but issues from an inner conviction. Pioneers such as Graham Howe, Jung, Alister Hardy, Laurens van der Post and others have extended the boundaries of man's thought, and consequently of man's experience. Along with this expansion of understanding and experience in the realm of philosophy and religion, the frontiers of knowledge in science and medicine are being shaken and enlarged.

In *The Frontiers of Science and Medicine*, edited by Rick J. Carlson, there are extracts from the May Lectures of 1974. Stuart Holroyd makes the final assessment. He was commissioned to do so by B.R.E.S., a journal published in the Netherlands, and I quote from his opening and closing paragraphs:

There are always men and women working at the frontiers of knowledge, suffering the derision and opprobrium of their peers, patiently pursuing their researches, biding their time. When fifty come together to exchange ideas and to pool the results of their researches, and when they can draw a paying audience of some eight hundred people every evening for a week to listen to them, they might justifiably feel that at last their time has come...

Knowledge and Wisdom

After presenting some surprising accounts and revolutionary ideas, Holroyd concludes:

> I imagine that this report will have tested the credulity threshold of most readers. What do you do with ideas that not only fall outside the scope of prevailing concepts of reality, but even invalidate them? What do you think of men whose ability and sincerity is indisputable, and who tell you that your science, your philosophy and your quotidian reality are partial and purblind? I personally have no answers. I am convinced by other contributors to the May Lectures that there is more to reality than meets the eye, and more than our Western science and philosophy comprehend. I am convinced that man has latent powers and enormous potentials for further evolution. But as regards psychic surgery, materialisations, dematerialisations and beings from outer space equipped with weird technologies, I just do not know; I can only say 'thank you' to Lyall Watson and Andrija Puharich for contributing to that state of enlightened mystification that may be the beginning of new knowledge.

A state of "enlightened mystification" may well prove to be more auspicious for growth and progress than rigid orthodoxy.

If we read and ponder on the lives of the Desert Fathers of the 4th Century AD, we find a surprisingly modern 'ring' in their bid for independence. It is not a revolt, but a determination to flee to the desert, to seek there direct experience in silence and isolation from controversy. Thomas Merton, in *The Wisdom of the Desert*, gives us a vivid impression of these early fathers, whose lives he describes and explains with great lucidity:

> The Desert Fathers did, in fact, meet the 'problems of their time' in the sense that *they* were among the few who were ahead of their time, and opened the way for the development of a new man and a new society...
> There was nothing to which they had to 'conform' except the secret, hidden, inscrutable will of God, which might differ very notably from one cell to another...
> The Fathers were humble and silent men, and did not have much to say. They replied to questions in a few words, to the point. Rather than give an abstract principle, they preferred to tell a concrete story. Their brevity is refreshing, and rich in content. There is more light and satisfaction in these laconic sayings than in many a long ascetic

treatise full of details about ascending from one 'degree' to another in the spiritual life. These words of the Fathers are never theoretical in our modern sense of the word. They are never abstract. They deal with concrete things and with jobs to be done in the everyday life of a 4th century monk. But what is said serves just as well for a 20th century thinker...

These Fathers distilled for themselves a very practical and unassuming wisdom, that is at once primitive and timeless, and which enables us to re-open the sources that have been polluted or blocked up altogether by the accumulated mental and spiritual refuse of our technological barbarism. Our time is in desperate need of this kind of simplicity. It needs to recapture some of the experience reflected in these lines. The word to emphasise is *experience*...

They were humble, quiet, sensible people, with a deep knowledge of human nature and enough understanding of the things of God to realise that they knew very little about Him. Hence they were not much disposed to make long speeches about the divine essence or even to declaim on the mystical meaning of scripture. If these men say little about God, it is because they know that when one has been somewhere close to His dwelling, silence makes more sense than a lot of words.

51

Knowledge and Wisdom

All through the *Verba Seniorum*, we find a repeated insistence on the primacy of love over everything else in the spiritual life: over knowledge, gnosis, asceticism, contemplation, solitude, prayer. Love in fact *is* the spiritual life, and without it all the other exercises of the spirit, however lofty, are emptied of content and become mere illusions. The more lofty they are, the more dangerous the illusion. Love, of course, means something much more than mere sentiment, much more than token favours and perfunctory almsdeeds. Love means an interior and spiritual identification with one's brother, so that he is not regarded as an 'object' to 'which' one 'does good'. The fact is that good done to another as to an object is of little or no spiritual value. Love takes one's neighbour as one's other self, and loves him with all the immense humility and discretion and reserve and reverence without which no one can presume to enter into the sanctuary of another's subjectivity. From such love, all authoritarian brutality, all exploitation, domineering and condescension must necessarily be absent...

Let it suffice for me to say that we need to learn from these men of the fourth century how to ignore prejudice, defy compulsion and strike out fearlessly into the unknown.

Knowledge and Wisdom

From the variety of stories in Merton's anthology, I quote but one:

Abbot Anastasius had a book written on very fine parchment which was worth eighteen pence, and had in it both Old and New Testaments in full. Once a certain brother came to visit him, and seeing the book made off with it. So that day when the Abbot Anastasius went to read his book, and found that it was gone, he realised that the brother had taken it. But he did not send after him to enquire about it for fear that the brother might add perjury to the theft. Well, the brother went down to the nearby city to sell the book. And the price he asked was sixteen pence. The buyer said: Give me the book that I may find out whether it is worth that much. With that the buyer took the book to the holy Anastasius and said: Father, take a look at this book, please, and tell me whether you think I ought to buy it for sixteen pence. Is it worth that much? Abbot Anastasius said: Yes, it is a fine book, it is worth that much. So the buyer went back to the brother and said: I showed the book to Abbot Anastasius, and he said it is a fine book and is worth sixteen pence. But the brother asked: Was that all he said? Did he make any other remarks? No, said the buyer, he did not say another word. Well, said the brother, I have

53

changed my mind and I don't want to sell this book after all. Then he hastened to Abbot Anastasius and begged him with tears to take back his book, but the Abbot would not accept it, saying: Go in peace, brother, I make you a present of it. But the brother said: If you do not take it back, I shall never have any peace. After that, the brother dwelt with the Abbot Anastasius for the rest of his life.

The wish to separate oneself from conflict and controversy and to seek inner harmony in silence seems to be the common experience of many seekers for knowledge and wisdom. There is perhaps another condition necessary, which is often stressed alike by poets and spiritual teachers. It is that ability to empty oneself of all prejudice — of preconceptions and of self-importance — and, in the words of Jesus, to 'become as a little child'. One of the most lovable and child-like of all the saints, Francis of Assisi, shows in his well-known prayer his understanding of the necessity to empty oneself of all negative thoughts and emotions, and to replace these with their opposite qualities:

Make me, O Lord, an instrument of thy peace.
Where there is hatred, may I bring love;
Where there is wrong, may I bring the spirit
of forgiveness;
Where there is error, may I bring truth;

Knowledge and Wisdom

Where there is despair, may I bring hope;
Where there are shadows, may I bring light;
Where there is sadness, may I bring joy.
Grant, Lord, that I may seek to comfort
                          rather than be comforted,
To understand rather than to be understood,
To love rather than to be loved,
For it is by giving that one receives;
It is by self-forgetting that one finds;
It is by forgiving that one is forgiven;
It is by dying that one awakens to eternal life.

The aspiration to become a clear channel for the 'wind of the spirit' has been expressed in many ways by many writers, but never more powerfully than by D.H. Lawrence in 'The Song of a Man Who Has Come Through':

Not I, not I, but the wind that blows through me!
A fine wind is blowing, the new direction of Time.
If only I let it bear me, carry me, if only it carry me!
If only I am sensitive, subtle, Oh, delicate, a
                          winged gift!
If only, most lovely of all, I yield myself and am
                          borrowed
By the fine, fine wind that takes its course through
                          the chaos of the world

Like a fine, an exquisite chisel, a wedge-blade
                  inserted;
If only I am keen and hard like the sheer tip
                  of a wedge
Driven by invisible blows,
The rock will split, we shall come at the wonder, we
                  shall find the Hesperides.
Oh, for the wonder that bubbles into my soul;
I would be a good fountain, a good well-head,
Would blur no whisper, spoil no expression.

    What is the knocking?
    What is the knocking at the door in the night?
    It is somebody wants to do us harm.

    No, no, it is the three strange angels.
    Admit them, admit them.

Here, surely, is a great New Age poem, expressing fearless, forward-looking expectancy in spite of the unknown — a necessary frame of mind as we cross the threshold into the uncharted country of the Aquarian Age. Studying, reading and re-reading Lawrence's words will be of more value than any amount of explanation or commentary.

A contemporary poet, who deserves to be better known and more widely read, has expressed similar

themes in one of her works. I quote from Thalia Gage's
'Prelude to Pentecost':

> It is not I, Lord, who sing
> But you who sing through me,
> I, but your voice, veiled and broken
> By words,
> But sometimes swinging down the long clear paths
> With your authentic signature of joy.

From long before the Christian era, poets and
writers have suggested, in a variety of ways, that the
whole of nature lies open before us, like a book for our
enlightenment. In certain moods, or perhaps more
accurately at certain levels of consciousness, we seem to
glimpse the truths which lie behind the visible world of
nature. Indeed, it is often the indescribable beauty of
nature which moves us so profoundly that we are
almost aware of the shift in the level of consciousness.
Wordsworth speaks of this experience in 'Tintern
Abbey' and his 'Ode on the Intimations of Immortality'. The mystical poet Thomas Traherne speaks of
his delight in 'rivers, meadows, woods and springs',
and of the deeper experience which comes 'from
viewing herbs and trees'.

> Observe those rich and glorious things;
> The rivers, meadows, woods and springs,

Knowledge and Wisdom

The fructifying sun;
To note from far
The rising of each twinkling star
For us his race to run.

A little child these well perceives,
Who, tumbling in green grass and leaves,
   May rich as kings be thought.
   But there's a sight
Which perfect manhood may delight,
   To which we shall be brought.

While in those pleasant paths we talk
'Tis that towards which at last we walk;
   For we may by degrees
   Wisely proceed
Pleasures of love and praise to heed,
   From viewing herbs and trees.

I.S. de Lubicz's book, *Her-Bak, Egyptian Initiate*, translated from the French by Sir Ronald Fraser, further illumines man's quest for wisdom on his journey through this life. As de Lubicz says, 'the events related take place between the twentieth and twenty-first dynasties in the temple of Karnak in face of the Theban mountains whose peaks dominate the Valley of the Kings'. The pupil Chick-pea chooses the way of knowledge, the mystical or gnostic way. The Sage gives him his name 'Her-Bak' and leads him to the temple:

> It was a year of fruitful studies. Her-Bak had the
> joy of breaking the seal of a new door that gave
> access to a more inward teaching...
>
> Her-Bak scanned the desert levels where gigantic
> pyramids stood over a city of tombs. The Sphinx,
> witness from very ancient times, watched over the
> secret of dead and living, pointing the one and the
> other to the Orient of resurrection. The disciple
> tried to count the temples they had seen during
> their pilgrimage. He sighed, 'I shall never remem-
> ber them all ... and we visited but few.'
>
> The Master gave their voyage its true signifi-
> cance. "All existence is a voyage in the course of
> which the soul, carried in its corporeal boat, is
> impregnated with consciousness as your eyes with
> the colours, your ears with the words, of nature.
> Thus do migrating birds. Each makes its flight in
> response to the vital call of its own being. One seeks
> the marshes, another Ra's beams; a third follows
> the ripening of the grain. Each one's path is
> governed by Ra's course, and by its own capacity
> for adaptation to changing conditions of land and
> climate. And on the journey its consciousness
> reawakens, enriched with fresh experience. Thus,
> your soul is an immortal wanderer in the short
> course of earth, the changes of the Dwat, the

glorious reaches of heaven. It isn't the number of
images received that counts, but the ineffaceable
impressions that enrich your consciousness, above
all the possibilities they awaken and bring out in
you. Remember the migratory birds. Each is called
by its desires and the aim of its existence. The aim
determines the journey."

From the time when the ancient wisdom was taught
to a selected few in the temples of Egypt up to the
present day, man has followed many teachers and
many paths in his quest for knowledge. A final goal is
always elusive. "Our greatest truths are but half
truths..." John Sparrow, a seventeenth-century herme-
ticist", suggests the mysterious nature of the spirit of
wisdom thus:

> The spirit of Wisdom cannot be delineated with
> a pen and ink, no more than a sound can be
> painted or the wind grasped in the hollow of the
> hand.

V

Tuning the Instrument here at the Door

Since I am coming to that Holy roome
Where, with thy Quire of Saints, for evermore
I shall be made thy music; as I come
I tune the instrument here at the door,
And what I must doe then, thinke here before.

These words by John Donne direct our attention to the very heart of the purpose of our life on this earth. They stir our imagination and provoke what Wordsworth calls 'obstinate questionings'. How are we to set about this tuning of our instrument, here in the ante-room of earth-life, before joining the great orchestra in the next dimension? Donne's powerful poetic imagery sets fire to our imagination. He is suggestive, not dogmatic, and we are left free to speculate and to undertake our own 'adventures in ideas'. Whatever our beliefs or prejudices about survival after physical death may be, we shall probably be familiar with the concept of many different levels of consciousness; and it is in this direction that we may find an interpretation of Donne's poem.

A wise teacher has said that even a little knowledge and understanding of the next sphere (for which we are all bound, whether we like it or not) will be of great value to us. If the next world is indeed largely a thought-world, Donne's words are fraught with a sense of urgency that underlines the spiritual law of cause and effect: as we think now, so shall we *be* when we discard the body. The metaphor of music, implying a vast orchestra in which we all participate, draws our attention to the possibility of unity in diversity, and to the underlying quality of harmony. Any orchestra would be the poorer if all the instruments were playing the same line of music: the secret lies in perfect blending. Implicit in Donne's image is the suggestion that each one of us will contribute a degree of harmony, or lack of it, according to the quality of thought and character built up through a possible succession of lives. "As a man thinketh in his heart, so is he." Harmonious blending, as we know is possible between individuals, may, in certain conditions, also function between the two worlds. Indeed, it has been said that no work of art or imagination is the work of one world only. Both the 'inspired guess' — that necessary part of the scientific method — as well as inspiration in the arts may well be the result of telepathic links between disincarnate and incarnate beings. Investigation and experiment lend support to this possibility.

There is much evidence that certain books, written within the last twenty-five years, are the result of prompting from disincarnate persons. In fact, the blending of disincarnate and incarnate thoughts seems both possible and effective. In Jane Sherwood's *Post Mortem Journal*, for example, we are offered a convincing picture of the condition to which a soul will pass after physical death, if he makes the transition in the conviction that death means extinction and that there is no afterlife. The account which comes to us through Jane Sherwood's writing identifies the communicator as T.E. Lawrence, and narrates Lawrence's story after his fatal motorcycle accident. I know of no better book for the reader approaching this subject for the first time and avid for some understanding about the transition called death. I quote from the last chapter, in which Lawrence reflects on the conditions of the world he now inhabits:

Earthly wisdom, I believe, has not got very far in analysing the process by which knowledge is obtained ... However it may be for earth, when I came here I soon found that my ways of apprehending and reasoning about things were very different ... The total reaction to all that is seen or heard — the keener awareness, the swifter response, involves the whole emotional being. For instance, when I see a bush or a tree I am not able to perceive it simply in visual terms: I have to reckon on an emotional response to it. I like it, I value it, or even love it, or if I am not yet beyond a negative response I may dislike it or even hate it; but there will be a strong feeling reaction in either case. Similarly with one's reactions to people. They awake the strongest responses of all. A cool, detached, merely intellectual reaction to anything is practically impossible while we are in this emotional body. We have to see, hear and understand with our feelings and this gives a keener and more personal edge to all impressions.

Donne's words — "And what I must doe then, think here before" — may well be echoing in our minds.

There is also impressive evidence to suggest that Professor F.W.H. Myers and his group of Cambridge friends — all already disincarnate — influenced Dr. Raynor Johnson, and helped him to write his book, *The Imprisoned Splendour.* Through the automatic writing of Geraldine Cummins, Johnson's old friend, Ambrose Pratt, imparts much relevant information, and goes on to offer him the task of writing another book embodying Douglas Fawcett's philosophy. This subsequently appeared as *Nurslings of Immortality*.

I quote from Johnson's work, *The Light and the Gate*, in which the important accounts are offered. From the next world, Ambrose Pratt informs Raynor Johnson as follows:

> After my passing, you longed to have a sign or some news of me. But the time was not ripe for the weaving of the pattern, as you will realise yourself. Neither you nor the times were ready. Action had to be delayed. But the desire for news of me remained latent in your consciousness. That faithful love eventually worked the miracle...
>
> I longed to speak to you at an earlier time. But I was only permitted to break the long silence in the appropriate season. In other words, the Group-soul creates the pattern for those who are members of it. It was designed that I should set you a certain task when you, in the measure of earth-time, were ripe for it.

Pratt goes on to give an account of how Myers and his group have succeeded in 'conveying ideas' into Johnson's mind:

> Occasionally the F.W.H. Myers group, which I shall henceforth call the Group, have conveyed

ideas to your deeper mind, or the general impulse which led you to write *The Imprisoned Splendour*. Now to prove to you that what I am saying to you is true, I must tell you that they have directed you of recent times to study Douglas Fawcett's philosophic works. In their view the one weakness in your own book was the philosophic section in it. Your finest achievement was that part which dealt with Mysticism. Your subconscious received a telepathic message which helped to lead you on through another to Fawcett's work...

Men do desire and are gropingly seeking, the Group tells me, for a fresh interpretation of the World system that harmonises with modern knowledge, and this, neither the accepted creeds nor academic philosophy are able to supply. Fawcett's philosophy reinforced by your scientific knowledge and your knowledge of the experimental work in psychical research, might well reconcile religion and science, put an end to their long conflict, and deal a fell blow to scientific materialism ... The Group have asked me to present you today with the conception of a new book, desire you to be the disciple or apostle of Fawcett...

This task offered to you is more important than anything else, so I beg of you to give it your serious consideration...

Tuning the Instrument here at the Door

In the following passage, Johnson comments on the script:

This most remarkable script gave me profound food for thought. It was forceful, authoritative and direct in its style: the work of a critical mind and intellect, offering me certain assurances, and inviting me (not abusing the position to command me) to do a task that had never crossed my mind. I knew nothing of a philosopher called Fawcett and his work. The name was vaguely familiar as that of an explorer who was lost on one of his expeditions. (Colonel Fawcett was in fact an older brother of Douglas Fawcett.) The statement ... that the Group 'have directed you of recent times to study Douglas Fawcett's philosophic works' was itself rather staggering. It was clearly a reference to the fact that a few weeks previously I had received a letter signed 'D. Fawcett'. The name meant nothing special to me: but the writer had read *The Imprisoned Splendour* and was writing an appreciative note of this book. He enclosed in this letter, however, a publisher's leaflet printed to advertise Fawcett's two books, *The Zermatt Dialogues* and *Oberland Dialogues*. He had written in his own hand on this leaflet, "I think these would interest you. They are a meeting of East and West." So it

was true that my attention had been drawn to
Fawcett's work!

The foregoing account of Raynor Johnson's telepathic link with Ambrose Pratt, Myers and his group
may well be one example of the possibility of the
blending of minds from the two worlds, a possibility of
a close partnership which exists and operates even now
far more often than is popularly supposed. It may well
become more widespread and more consciously
understood as we move into the Aquarian Age.

Rudolf Steiner writes with authority about a time
when human beings were neither limited by sense
perception nor separated from the spirit world, but
lived in conscious communication with it. In *The
Apocalypse of Saint John,* Steiner interprets the significance of the Atlantean Epoch, and throws a new light
on the well-known story of the Great Flood:

Most human beings of that epoch were capable of
developing a certain dim kind of clairvoyance.
They were not limited to the physical sense world;
they lived among divine spiritual beings; they saw
these divine spiritual beings around them. In the
transition from the Atlantean to the post-Atlantean
epoch, man's vision was cut off from the spiritual,
astral and etheric worlds and limited to his physical
world. In the first post-Atlantean age of civilisation,

men were possessed by a great longing for what
their ancestors had seen in ancient Atlantis, on
which, however, the door had closed. Our ancestors
saw the ancient wisdom with their own spiritual
eyes, though dimly. They lived among spirits, they
had intercourse with gods and spirits. Such was the
feeling of those who belonged to that ancient
sacred Indian civilisation; they longed with all their
might to look back and see what their forefathers
had seen, and of which the ancient wisdom spoke...

Steiner then proceeds to compare this era with our
own:

We are living in an age when man is actually the
slave of outer conditions ... The deep descent
below the sphere of the human has only just come
about. In our age, the mind has become the slave
of matter. An enormous amount of mental energy
has been used in our age to penetrate the natural
forces in the outer world for the purpose of making
this outer world as comfortable a place as possible
for man...

Nevertheless, Steiner is optimistic. He foresees a time
when true spiritual teaching will be understood and
followed.

Christian life is only now beginning to develop. In the future it will rise to a transcendent glory, because only then will humanity understand the Gospels. When these are fully understood it will be seen what an enormous amount of spiritual life they contain. The more they are disseminated in their true form, the more will it be possible for humanity, in spite of all material culture, to develop a spiritual life and rise again into spiritual worlds.

At present, however, we are still far from that time. In *The Divine Flame,* Sir Alister Hardy asks the question:

Would Jesus himself be a Christian? If by the term Christian we mean what so many orthodox churchmen appear to mean, then I, for one, very much doubt it ... To me Jesus speaks of reality — the most brilliant burning of the divine flame in all history. Yet I find so much in orthodox Christianity that repels me.

It must be remembered that Steiner was both a scientist of world-wide reputation and also a man of unusual spiritual gifts. His ideas seem to illuminate the more shadowy utterances of mystics through the centuries, who suggest that man in his primal state was at one with God. After the fall, there follows the long

journey home, from separation to unity. We find
echoes of this theme, which seems to haunt man, in
countless legends and myths. And this magnificent
verse of a hymn written by Peter Abelard in the twelfth
century also expresses symbolically man's journey back
to his source. Abelard uses as an allegory the exile of
the Jews to Babylon and the return to Jerusalem:

> Nostrum est interim mentes erigere,
> Et totis patriam votis appetere,
> Et ad Ierusalem a Babylonia
> Post longa regredi tandem exilia,

The verse in the well-known English translation of the
hymn does not really give the exact meaning of the
original Latin. Here is another translation, which
renders more precisely the sense of Abelard's words:

> Meanwhile, our summons is, Lift up your hearts,
> With soul, mind, body seek your Fatherland,
> And to Jerusalem from Babylon,
> Long exile over, there return at last.

In *The Old Stones of Land's End*, John Michell
expresses ideas similar to Steiner's about a time when
man became separated from the gods and his daily
dependence on communication with them. Michell
explains how his study of old stones near Land's End

brought him to consider philosophies and approaches
to cosmology very different from those usually held
today:

The modern approach to cosmology is physical
and analytical and our science is directed accord-
ingly; but the science of the megalith builders was
required to deal with a different state of affairs, a
world populated by gods, spirits and shades of the
dead...
Having begun with modest proposals to investi-
gate the old stones near Land's End, we have come
inevitably to face the grand prospect of seeking
initiation into the secrets of the ancient world; and
the delightful feature of this study is that it is not
concerned with an arbitrary system of thought,
invented in response to the temporary circumstances of a particular historical period, but
something that is essential in human nature and
finally inseparable from settled human existence.
The orthodox view of the world, held universally
in all ages and by all lasting civilisations, is as
expressed in Jung's interpretation of Basilius
Valentinus:
"The earth is not a dead body, but is inhabited
by a spirit that is its life and soul. All created
things, minerals included, draw their strength
from the earth-spirit. This spirit is life, it is

nourished by the stars, and it gives nourishment to all the living things it shelters in its womb. Through the spirit received from on high, the earth hatches the minerals in her womb as the mother her unborn child.''

This philosophy has long outlived the active science by which it was once implemented, but if the above statement is compared with the properties so far discovered of megalithic sites, the connection is apparent. Since the earth is an organism, a planetary being, its health and contentment are naturally reflected in the welfare of its inhabitants, of whom only the human race has the intelligence to be consciously aware of this. Behind all ancient cosmology, from the earliest traditions of China and the East to the mysticism of the Neo-Platonists, is the appreciation, realistic and unsentimental, of human dependence on the elemental gods, personifications of cosmic and terrestrial forces. The fortunes of men, the benevolence or otherwise of their environment, varies in accordance with the degree of harmony between the divine entities...

The megalithic revolution took place at a period when the archaic way of life, the wandering, divinely inspired existence of the 'golden age' was becoming abandoned for agricultural and settled communities. Like all migrant people, the early inhabitants of Britain moved about the country in regular orbit, treading the same paths they had followed 'from the beginning of time', visiting at the appropriate seasons the sacred places on their circuit. They had no religion as such, no philosophy, science, magic or art as distinguished from the normal acitivites of life. The spirit of the earth was their guide, the local deities their familiars...

With settlement the primordial rhythm was lost. People no longer travelled by the stars and followed the veins of the earth to the old landmarks. Contact with the gods, formerly incessant, now ceased. In its place grew up a host of substitutes, theology, philosophy, the arts, sciences and magic. Moral codes replaced the old codes of necessity; the journey was ritualised in fasts, pilgrimages, ceremonies and invocations. However, despite the comforts of the settled existence, the uneasy feeling remains that in abandoning the nomadic ways men are no longer following the life for which they were created...

The gravest consequence of the settled life is loss of contact with the local gods and ancestral spirits, by whom every age in the cyclical journey was formerly attended. These inhabited certain shrines, places to which the old wandering people returned at regular yearly intervals, guided there by the configuration of the stars and the landmarks on the horizon. This was their sacred duty, for the ancient travellers were not only in their movements imitating the planetary orbits, but, in their belief, were themselves an essential part of the cosmic order. The creation of the world was seen as an everlasting process, in which certain places in the landscape and the spirits that frequented them played an active part. In them was the source of all divine gifts, of natural fertility, of health and rebirth and of the inspired oracles by which the people were governed. At the appropriate place and season the god revealed his presence in the phenomena of nature and his will in visions, dreams and omens.

Now, separated by thousands of years from the 'wandering, divinely inspired existence of the Golden Age' described by John Michell, Walt Whitman's words resonate with singular relevance:

I see something of God each hour of the
    twenty-four, and each moment then,
In the faces of men and women I see God, and in
    my own face in the glass,
I find letters from God dropt in the street and every
    one is signed by God's name,

And I leave them where they are, for I know that
  whereso'ere I go,
Others will punctually come for ever and ever.

Megalithic man sought revelations from the invisible
world through visions, omens and dreams. In the same
way nowadays, poets like Walt Whitman and A.E. and
writers like Laurens van der Post and Allan
McGlashan indicate something of their experience
with the supersensory world. In *The Savage and
Beautiful Country*, for example, Alan McGlashen
urges us to pay more attention to our dreams:

> Is it not possible that the Dreamer, this myster-
> ious Guest who lodges uninvited in the psyche of
> every man — and, for all we know, of every living
> thing — may be one of the 'common but elusive'
> factors which link us to other and high-dimensional
> forms of existence? ... Is it not possible?
> The second question, or rather the second half of
> the same question — *to whom is the Dreamer
> talking?* — leads us into still more peculiar paths of
> thought. It gives one the same baffled, slightly
> disquieting feeling that I used to create deliberately
> as a child — no doubt as many children do — by
> gazing at myself in a mirror until a moment came
> when I could not decide whether I was looking at
> my reflection or my reflection was looking at me.

My sense of identity, my 'I'-ness, came out from its unknown hiding-place and hovered between me and my reflection in a way that was at once frightening and fascinating. It was, I suppose, a kind of childish invocation of the *I-Thou* mystery. Perhaps Chouang-Chou put himself in the same state some two thousand years ago, on waking up from his famous dream that he was a butterfly, and asking himself whether he was in reality a man who had dreamed he was a butterfly, or a butterfly now dreaming that it was a man.

But to return: here is the dreaming mind night upon night, like Scheherazade, spinning its lovely, meaningful yet perplexing tales — for *someone*, surely? Do 'I' dream my dreams? And if so, am I merely chattering to myself as children do? Jung ... says No: that 'we ' do not dream our dreams, but that dreams happen to us in the same way that experiences in everyday life happen to us. The African Bushman, still cocooned in his Stone Age wisdom, goes farther. Of human life as a whole he says surprisingly — "There is a dreamer dreaming us."

If Stone-Age man and this great modern are right, the Dreamer may be some *supra-personal mode of experiencing*, and the dream process, when attended to by the conscious mind, may be a form of colloquy between the personal and the super-personal. On this hypothesis the Dreamer is talking to the conscious mind, the Ego. It is trying to awake the Ego to those factors in the total situation which lie outside the Ego's range, and which the Ego could never arrive at by its own efforts, however far the conscious mind *at its existing level* were developed.

This last admission could be the crucial act of humility demanded of the conscious mind if it is to pass beyond its present frontiers...

But not all educated minds have rejected the Dreamer's power to solve intellectually insoluble problems. There are men of outstanding genius who have deliberately and successfully sought its aid, and others of equal calibre who have gratefully acknowledged its unexpected assistance. Poincaré, the French mathematician, himself recorded that when faced with a problem which defeated his most determined conscious efforts, he would go to sleep in the hope, frequently justified, that the dreaming mind would find the solution. James Brindley, the great engineer, when confronted with an unusually difficult question, used to go to bed until it was solved. Kekulé, Professor of Chemistry in Ghent, whose major discovery has been called 'the most brilliant piece of prediction in the whole range of organic chemistry', was given the vital clue to this discovery by a vision of circling atoms which appeared to him in a dream. In describing this occurrence to a scientific congress, he ended with the words — *"Let us learn to dream, gentlemen."* These random examples are drawn from Arthur Koestler's remarkable book, *The Act of Creation*, in which he records, in strictly attested detail, many similar illustrations of the value — if not indeed the necessity — co-opting the Dreamer when attempting to solve the apparently insoluble. Koestler himself believes that the essence of discovery is the unlikely marriage of previously unrelated things ... and the ultimate match-maker is the Unconscious. The acknowledgments of such men cannot, I suggest, be lightly disregarded.

In his recent book on Jung, Laurens van der Post writes of the mystery of the dream process:

Mystery includes the known as well as the unknown; the ordinary as well as the extraordinary. Once the feeling of mystery abandons our travel-stained senses in contemplation of the same well-worn scene, we have ceased, in some vital sense, to know what we are observing. What that mystery is, is beyond verbal definition. We know only that its effect on us is either positive or negative. It is, perhaps, most creatively, the feeling that in the midst of our own partial knowing and experience

79

of life there is a presence of something far greater than man can comprehend. Reality, no matter how widened and heightened our perceptions, never ceases to be an infinite mystery. Again, Shakespeare expresses it better than anyone else when he makes the doomed Lear say to Cordelia, "We shall take upon us the mystery of things and be God's spies." In other words, awareness of the mystery of things acknowledged and revered, though inexpressible and utterly non-rational, is also a vital form of knowing which enables the human spirit to pass through the defence lines of what he knows, and enter into the embattled territory of the unknown like a spy to prepare the way for the mobilised forms of consciousness to follow and so extend the area of his awareness. And it is in all these senses that this ever-recurrent process of the dream, the longing in its keeping and the consciousness which emerges from it, is one of the most moving and life-giving aspects of the mystery that motivates our brittle lives.

As we come to the end of this last section, we may consider what conditions seem essential, or likely to be of assistance, for 'tuning the instrument here at the door'. Perhaps it is natural to put first a burning desire to find the 'Conductor of the Orchestra', or at least to search untiringly for one. As St. Exupéry says, "Let a man in a garret burn with enough intensity and he will set fire to the world." This quality of steadfast, sustained, unextinguishable perseverance seems as essential as another quality, that of unqualified generosity, a spontaneous self-giving which becomes a pulse of life and not a thought-out policy. Graham Howe, in *The Mind of the Druid*, expresses this state of giving without counting the cost:

> We learn one lesson from the seed that diamonds have never taught us. For seeds, unlike diamonds, are for spending — for throwing away, almost. For unless the seed falls into the ground, dying buried in the darkness of the earth for due season, there can be no spring nor harvest. The image of the seed is the living message of truth for all of us: that death of some kind is the cause of all renewal. 'Death', albeit in inverted commas, is a cause; and life its consequence. Thus sleep is a little death: but so are looking and listening, which require a condition of self-emptying, or 'dying to know', before communication from the other can be received. So, 'expiring' with every breath, we may grow continuously, until the time arrives when we must all experience the irreversible state of change, called death.

81

Tuning the Instrument here at the Door

Closely allied to this quality of fearless giving, and in part motivating it, is the power of love — a word so misused and debased these days that it needs serious re-thinking. I know of no better way of clarifying it than by quoting a short passage from Juan Mascaro's 'Introduction' to *The Bhagavad Gita:*

> The true progress of man on earth is the progress of an inner vision. We have a progress in science, but is it in harmony with spiritual progress? We want a scientific progress, but do we want a moral progress? It is not enough to have more, or even to know more, but to live more, and if we want to live more we must learn to love more. Love is the 'treasure hid in a field', and this field according to the *Gita* is our own soul. Here the treasure is found for which the wise merchant 'went and sold all he had'. And contrary to the law of matter where to give more means to have less, in the law of love the more one gives the more one has.

This theme is echoed in the *Tao Tê Ching:*

> He who loves does not dispute:
> He who disputes does not love...
> The sage treasures nothing for himself; and yet
> The more he spends, the more he earns;
> The more he gives, the more he has...

How often we agree theoretically with these
sentiments, yet how seldom do we dare to live by
them — to put them into practice. It seems there is
a whole area of unrealised, untapped potential within
us, would we but believe it.

> O, the fabulous wings unused
> Folded in the heart!

This cry, uttered in Christopher Fry's play, *A Sleep of
Prisoners*, comes almost as a shock of discovery, and we
are "surprised by joy".

Then as we ponder again on Donne's words — "And
what we must do then think here before" — they
become charged with expanding meaning. The capital
importance of the power of thought becomes increasingly clear. The words of the Book of Proverbs — "As a
man thinketh in his heart, so is he" — assume a new
significance. In *The Descent of Man*, Charles Darwin
supports this view:

> The highest possible stage of moral culture is
> when we recognise that we ought to control our
> thoughts.

The Buddha teaches that all we are is the result of
what we have thought. And so it follows that what we
think now will determine what kind of music 'we

become' when we discard the limitations of the body and experience that life is continous. To tune ourselves in to peace and harmony will become almost instinctive, and disputation and argument will be revealed as not only useless, but harmful. I quote from a Greek Franciscan:

> Those who fought for the opposing views had become somewhat deranged by over-scrutiny of the mysteries of God.

Here again, a verse from the *Tao Tê Ching* indicates the way towards harmony:

> Gentle water is tender and yielding,
> The most humble of things under heaven;
> But see, how it conquers the rock!
> 'The tender overcomes the hard.
> The gentle overcomes the strong.'
> This is a truth that all men know;
> But how few men live their lives in this truth!

Writing on 'Regeneration' at the end of the 16th Century, Jakob Boehme has this to say:

> Therefore I say, that whatsoever fighteth and contendeth about the letter is all *Babel*. The letters of the Word proceed from, and stand all in, one

84

root, which is the Spirit of God; as the various flowers stand all in the earth and grow about one another. They fight not with one another about their differences of colour, smell, and taste, but suffer the sun, the rain, the wind, the heat, and cold to do with them as they please; and yet everyone of them groweth in its own peculiar essence and property.

Even so it is with the children of God. They have various gifts and degrees of knowledge, yet all from one Spirit. They all rejoice at the great wonders of God, and give thanks to the most High in his wisdom. Why then should they contend about him *in whom they live and have their being*, and of whose substance they themselves are.

It is the greatest folly that is in *Babel* for people to strive about religion, as the devil hath made the world to do; so that they contend vehemently about opinions of their own forging, about the letter, when the Kingdom of God consisteth of no opinion, but in power and love.

Again, Juan Mascaro's 'Introduction' to *The Bhagavad Gita* serves to illuminate our theme:

The spiritual visions of man confirm and illuminate each other ... Great poems in different languages have different values but they are all

85

poetry, and the spiritual visions of man come all from One Light. In them we have Lamps of Fire that burn to the glory of God.

The following passage comes from Ralph Waldo Trine's book, *In Tune with the Infinite:*

Let there be many windows in your soul,
That all the glory of the universe
May beautify it. Not the narrow pane
Of one poor creed can catch the radiant rays
That shine from countless sources. Tear away
The blinds of superstition; let the light
Pour through fair windows, broad as truth itself
And high as heaven ... Tune your ear
To all the worldless music of the stars
And to the voice of nature, and your heart
Shall turn to truth and goodness as the plant
Turns to the sun. A thousand unseen hands
Reach down to help you to their peace-crowned
                              heights,
And all the forces of the firmament
Shall fortify your strength. Be not afraid
To thrust aside half-truths and grasp the whole.

These thoughts of Trine's lead us back full circle to Earl Balfour's words quoted in Chapter I, "Our greatest truths are but half-truths..." We are exhorted to use them 'as a tent in which to pass a summer night' — and to remember that we are on the move, ready for further exploration and new discovery.

Man is in a state of 'becoming', with potentials and latent possibilities greater than are generally imagined. Will he use his God-like gifts for good or evil? Will he continue to pursue happiness by seeking material gain, thus fostering competition and selfishness? Or will he perceive his spiritual nature, and discover that material gain as a goal is not only empty and worthless, but brings with it a climate of fear and greed which in turn breeds hatred and war? Looking only outwards, at evidence in the exterior world today, many would answer these questions with deep pessimism and sad disillusion. But as I write these last words, I remember a stone carving over the West Porch of Chartres Cathedral. A curious little figure looks down from amongst his geometrical instruments. It is Pythagoras. His words, coming to us across twenty-five centuries, shall be the last. They are these:

"Take courage, for the human race is divine."

Pierce thy Heart
to Find the Key

Behind this section of our anthology, there is a specific purpose — to gather together a number of poems which express the spiritual world-view so powerfully emerging in our time. In the pages that follow, I include quotations cited in courses at Attingham Park and in Wrekin Trust conferences and lectures. On these occasions, students have often asked for copies of the statements in question. Here they are, therefore, with brief commentary and interpretation where necessary. In no sense is this an attempt to definitively cover the entire field. It is, rather, a random selection of poetry which speaks for me the truth and vision for which we strive in the birth of the New Age.

The rising tide of a new spiritual understanding is one of the notable phenomena in the intellectual climate of our time. Basically, it implies a reversal of the materialistic perspective, and it brings with it an inner certainty that the universe is a great living presence, shot through with Creative Intelligence. Cold intellect can dissect and analyse matter and energy and thus offer us a part of the total picture. Heightened imagination can apprehend the living whole, and this is the faculty that makes a poet.

Deep within its own nature, the soul knows that it belongs to a world of light, a higher finer realm interpenetrating the world of physical form. This plane of being is invisible to the five senses which are attuned only to external forms, but it is no less a reality. When contacted by the subtler senses, a profound joy is experienced and an inner certainty of truth. This brings a conviction that the way has been found and the goal is being validly approached. It is just such oneness of being that the poetic consciousness apprehends; and it is with that aspect of poetic expression that we are now concerned.

Wordsworth reflects the longing of the soul — its nostalgia for the realm from which it is increasingly divorced through intellectual materialism. Let us therefore commence our selection with one of his great sonnets:

The world is too much with us; late and soon,
Getting and spending, we lay waste our powers;
Little we see in nature that is ours,

We have given our hearts away, a sordid boon!
This sea that bares her bosom to the moon;
The winds that will be howling at all hours,
And are up-gathered now like sleeping flowers;
For this, for everything, we are out of tune,
It moves us not. — Great God! I'd rather be
A pagan suckled in a creed outworn,
So might I, standing on this pleasant lea,
Have glimpses that would make me less forlorn;
Have sight of Proteus rising from the sea,
Or hear old Triton blow his wreathèd horn.

Wordsworth had the gift of inner vision into the
'etheric' world which vitalises and animates the whole
of nature, and for many of us in our youth the faculties
for perception of this realm are still active.

There was a time when meadow, grove,
And stream,
The earth, and every common sight,
To me did seem
Apparelled in celestial light,
The glory and the freshness of a dream.
It is not now as it hath been of yore, —
Turn whersoe'er I may,
By night or day,
The things which I have seen I now can see no more.

In the famous lines composed at Tintern Abbey, the youthful glory is replaced by a deeper experience:

> ... And I have felt
> A presence that disturbs me with the joy
> Of elevated thoughts; a sense sublime
> Of something far more deeply interfused,
> Whose dwelling is the light of setting suns,
> And the round ocean and the living air,
> And the blue sky, and in the mind of man:
> A motion and a spirit, that impels
> All thinking things, all objects of all thought,
> And rolls through all things.

The widening of understanding to blend with the living wholeness of the world is the inner goal and striving of the coming age. Therefore, poetry and the poetic experience take on a new significance for us; for if we can work our consciousness into the crystallised form of the poem, we may ourselves touch the deeper experience of wonder. This possibility is expressed by Anna Kingsford in the following lines:

The poet hath no self apart from his larger Self. His personality is Divine; and being Divine it hath no limits.

He is supreme and ubiquitous in consciousness; his heart beats in every element.

The pulses of the infinite Deep of Heaven vibrate in

his own; and responding to their strength and their plenitude, he feels more intensely than other men.

Not merely he sees and examines these Rocks and Trees; these variable waters and these glittering peaks.

Not merely he hears this plaintive wind, these rolling peals.

But he is all these, and when he sings, it is not he — the Man — whose voice is heard; it is the voice of all Manifold Nature herself.

In his voice the Sunshine laughs; the Mountains give forth their sonorous Echoes: The swift lightnings flash.

The great continual Cadence of Universal Life moves and becomes articulate in human language.

O Joy profound! O boundless Selfhood! O God-like personality! All the Gold of the Sunset is thine: the Pillars of Chrysolite; the purple vault of Immensity!

The daughters of Earth love thee: the Water-nymphs tell thee their secrets; thou knowest the Spirit of all silent things.

Sunbeams are thy Laughter, and the Raindrops of Heaven are thy Tears; in the wrath of the Storm thy Heart is shaken; and thy Prayer goeth up with the Wind unto God.

Thou art multiplied in the Conscience of all living creatures; because thou only understandest, among the Sons of Men.

As Rupert Brooke said, we are

Pierce thy Heart to Find the Key

A pulse of the eternal mind, no less.

And Sir Donald Tovey once defined genius as

The most effective channel for the Creative Source.

Indeed, we belong to these eternal worlds, and to find our way back to them is the goal of the soul's awakening. After the experience of separation by the drastic limitation of incarnation in a physical body, we can enmember ourselves again with the great Oneness. This longing and this hope are expressed by Francis Thompson in 'The Mistress of Vision', of which I quote only a few lines. The soul speaks and the answer comes from the higher self:

> Where is the land of Luthany,
> Where is the tract of Elenore?
> I am bound therefor.
>
> 'Pierce thy heart to find the key;
> With thee take
> Only what none else would keep:
> Learn to dream when thou dost wake,
> Learn to wake when thou dost sleep . . .
> When thy seeing blindeth thee
> To what thy fellow mortals see,
> When their sight to thee is sightless;
> Their living, death; their light, most lightless;

Search no more —
Pass the gates of Luthany, tread the region Elenore.'

Where is the land of Luthany,
And where the region Elenore?
I do faint therefor.

'When to the new eyes of thee
All things by immortal power
Near or far,
Hiddenly
To each other linkèd are,
That thou canst not stir a flower
Without troubling of a star;
..... Seek no more,
O seek no more!
Pass the gates of Luthany, tread the region Elenore.'

It is , of course, easy to say this feelingly, but the thought must not be allowed to masquerade as the real experience — which for most of us can only be a remote goal. But the goal and the way are closely united, and the first essential is to grasp the concept of a wholeness of which we are an integral part. In *Jerusalem* (Chapter 1), William Blake, that great prophet of the New Age, speaks of his purpose as teacher, artist and poet:

... I rest not from my great task!
To open the Eternal Worlds, to open the
   immortal Eyes
Of Man inwards into the Worlds of Thought,
   into Eternity
Ever expanding in the Bosom of God, the
   Human Imagination.
O Saviour, pour upon me thy Spirit of meekness
   and love!
Annihilate the Selfhood in me; be thou all
   my life!

And, as Blake states in prose:

> This world of Imagination is the world of Eternity.
> It is the bosom into which we shall go after the death
> of the vegetated body. This world of Imagination is
> Infinite and Eternal, whereas the world of genera-
> tion and vegetation is finite and temporal. All
> things are comprehended in their Eternal Forms in
> the divine body of the Saviour, the true voice of
> Eternity, the Human Imagination.

Coleridge defined imagination as:

> the repetition in the finite mind of the eternal act
> of creation in the infinite I AM.

Keats said:

> I am certain of nothing but the holiness of the heart's affection and the truth of Imagination.

And Shelley:

> Poetry is the breath and finer spirit of all knowledge. It is the impassioned expression on the face of science.

It is indeed a great marvel and paradox that, by entering inwards, we can move through, and so discover that our consciousness can indeed expand to encompass the breadth of the universe. As Andrew Glazewski used to say:

> Your consciousness is not in your body: Your body is in your consciousness.

Charles James Earle expresses this important principle in his sonnet 'Bodily Extension':

> The body is not bounded by its skin;
>   Its effluence, like a gentle cloud of scent,
>   Is wide into the air diffused, and blent
> With elements unseen, its way doth win,
> To ether frontiers where take origin

96

Pierce thy Heart to Find the Key

Far subtler systems, nobler regions meant
To be the area and the instrument
Of operations ever to begin
Anew and never end. Thus every man
Wears as his robe the garment of the sky —
So close his union with the cosmic plan
So perfectly he pierces low and high
Reaching as far in space as creature can
And co-extending with immensity.

Note the 'ether frontiers' which we must cross. Our rockets are fired for the exploration of physical space, but there is another form of space exploration in the expansion of consciousness. To this, there can be no end. We are beginning to explore the frequency bands and up into subtler systems, reaching like Dante towards the Empyrean. Modern spiritual research has familiarised us with that field of unified vital energies and forces which plays with infinite diversity into every form, and holds together the particles comprising visible objects in all the kingdoms of nature. But cold intellect alone cannot attain the experience of this all-pervading unity. It can study the form, but the being within the form remains inaccessible to it.

We must awaken in ourselves the dormant faculties of higher perception. This involves the development of subtler senses. If we are to begin to experience the reality of higher realities, we must discover and employ the inner eye, the inner power of listening, a subtler sense of thought. For the five accepted senses are really filters to protect man from the power of the universe. The soul in incarnation takes upon itself the protective sheaths of the physical, etheric and astral bodies in order to function effectively in the density of earth's gravity-field. We might compare it to a diver donning a heavy diving suit in order to explore the wonders at the bottom of the sea. Another metaphor is provided by Martin Armstrong in 'The Cage':

> Man, afraid to be alive
> Shuts his soul in senses five
> From fields of uncreated light
> Into the crystal tower of sight,
> And from the roaring songs of space
> Into the small flesh-carven place
> Of the ear whose cave impounds
> Only small and broken sounds,
> And to his narrow sense of touch
> From strength that held the stars in clutch,
> And from the warm ambrosial spice
> Of flowers and fruits of paradise,
> Into the frail and fitful power
> Of scent and tasting, sweet and sour;
> And toiling for a sordid wage
> There is his self-created cage

Ah, how safely barred is he
From menace of Eternity.

Birth is indeed to be seen as a descent of a free-ranging spiritual being into the severe limitations of the body; and we shall learn to see death as truly a rebirth and release into a plane of light. To appreciate this, we must overcome the natural identification with our lower self and awaken to the great truth that we possess a self that is higher — a spiritual member of our greater being. This appreciation is the gateway to an experience of ourselves as participating in the whole. It is the true 're-membering'. For the New Age vision is re-establishing man as a being of spirit, soul and body; and we may be certain that a droplet of divinity cannot be extinguished by the discarding of the worn-out body.

Here is a verse from Edmund Spenser:

So every spirit as it is more pure
And hath in it the more of heavenly light
So it the fairer body doth procure
To habit in, and it more fairly dight
With cheerful grace and amiable sight,
For of the soul the body form doth take
And soul is form and doth the body make.

In the same connection, it is worth considering
Coleridge's 'Religious Musings':

There is one mind, one omnipresent Mind
Omnific. His most holy name is Love.
Truth of subliming import...
        'Tis the sublime in man,
Our noontide Majesty, to know ourselves
Parts and proportions of one wondrous whole.
This fraternises man.......

        Toy bewitched,
Made blind by lusts, disinherited of soul,
No common centre Man, no common sire
Knoweth! A sordid solitary thing
Mid countless brethren with a lonely heart
Through courts and cities the smooth savage roams,
Feeling himself, his own low self, the whole;
When he by sacred sympathy might make
The Whole one Self! Self that no alien knows,
Self, far diffused as fancy's wing can travel.
Self, spreading still! Oblivious of its own
Yet all of all possessing. This is Faith.
This the Messiah's destined victory.

What a picture of modern men! Indeed, in our
heathen culture we can be 'smooth savages'. But
'sacred sympathy', the ability to widen and intensify

imaginative thinking, leads to the discovery of the divinity within all created things and our affinity with the being within all form. Thus we are led out of loneliness — a necessary phase in the development of self-awareness — to the discovery of our higher self which is the gateway to wholeness. Herein lies the triumphant challenge of the last line. It is the destined victory of the higher powers that we should each widen consciousness to find that our inner being is truly united with all life. Then we shall be able to say with Traherne:

> You will never enjoy the world aright till the sea itself floweth in your veins, till you are clothed with heavens and crowned with the stars; and perceive yourself to be the sole heir of the whole world, and more than so, because men are in it who are every one the sole heir as well as you...

The works of Thomas Traherne, who died in 1674, were lost and not rediscovered until the first decade of this century. In a sense, that is appropriate, for only now can his vision be truly understood. Traherne possessed the capacity to remember back into the womb and beyond, and most of his writing strives to impart the living experience of oneness with the divinity in all created things. The great discovery we are now making is that the void or centre we enter in

101

meditation is indeed the magic portal through which
we can pass into the eternal worlds. This is expressed
by the poem, 'My Spirit', in which Traherne struggles
with the great paradox of the inner centre which is, at
the same time, infinite. I quote from the closing
stanzas:

> My essence was capacity
>   That felt all things...
> That made me present evermore
>   With whatsoe'er I saw.
> An object, if it were before
> My eye, was by Dame Nature's law
>   Within my soul.
>
> ..... A strange mysterious sphere,
>   A deep abyss
>   That sees and is
> The only proper place of Heavenly Bliss.
> A strange extended orb of Joy
>   Proceeding from within.
> Which did on every side, convey
> Itself, and being nigh of kin
>   To God, did every way
> Dilate itself even in an instant, and
> Like an indivisible centre stand
> At once surrounding all eternity.
>   'Twas not a sphere

   Yet did appear
One infinite...
'Twas not a sphere, but 'twas a might
Invisible and yet gave light.

O wondrous Self! O sphere of light
   O sphere of joy most fair
O act, O power infinite;
   O subtile and unbounded air!
      O living orb of sight!
Thou which within me art, yet me! Thou eye
And temple of His whole infinity!
   O what a world art thou! A world within!
      All things appear,
      All objects are
Alive in Thee! Supersubstantial, rare
   Above themselves, and nigh of kin
      To those pure things we find
         In His great mind
Who made the world! Tho' now eclipsed by sin,
   There they are useful and divine,
Exalted where they ought to shine.

In 'The Praeparative', Traherne describes the
experience of pre-existence. This principle is of the
utmost importance to us today. As we have noted, the
imperishable spiritual entity survives death, for an
eternal spiritual being cannot be extinguished. But

that we existed as a developed soul before birth is a most vital point if we are to understand the meaning of earth-life. Traherne first clearly describes the embryo:

> ... Before I skill'd to prize
>   Those living Stars, mine Eys;
> Before, I knew these Hands were mine
> Or that my sinews did my Members join...
>   I was within
> A House I knew not, newly cloath'd with skin.

> Then was my Soul my only All to me,
>   A living endless Eye
>   Scarce bounded with the Sky
> Whose Power and Act and Essence was to see;
>   I was an inward sphere of Light
> Or an interminable Orb of Sight
>   Exceeding that which makes the days,
> A Vital Sun, that shed abroad its rays,
>   All Life, all Sense,
> A naked, simple, pure, intelligence.

What a challenge to parents, doctors and teachers! We should indeed never think of the new-born child as a tiny soul, but as a mature soul beginning the drastic descent into a tiny frame. Wordsworth expresses a similar vision in his great 'Ode: Intimations of Immortality from Recollections of Early Childhood':

Pierce thy Heart to Find the Key

Our birth is but a sleep and a forgetting:
The Soul that rises with us, our life's Star,
   Hath had elsewhere its setting,
   And cometh from afar;
   Not in entire forgetfulness,
   And not in utter nakedness,
But trailing clouds of glory do we come
   From God, who is our home:
Heaven lies about us in our infancy!
Shades of the prison-house begin to close
   Upon the growing Boy,
But He beholds the light, and whence it flows,
   He sees it in his joy;
The Youth, who daily farther from the east
   Must travel, still is Nature's Priest,
   And by the vision splendid
   Is on his way attended;
At length the Man perceives it die away,
And fade into the light of common day.

When this process occurs, we tend too easily to assume
that the earlier light was an illusion. But surely it is for
each of us, in his maturing years, to revive the 'vision
splendid'. The all-important principle is that there is
no renewal without a dying process, no death without a
sequel of becoming and resurrection. As Goethe puts it
is 'Selige Sehnsucht' ('The Soul's Yearning'):

Und solang Du das nicht hast
Dieses: Stirb und werde!
Bist Du nur ein trüber Gast
Auf der dunklen Erde.

(And so long as this you lack,
This dying and becoming,
You are but a dull guest
On the darkling earth.)

William Butler Yeats was similarly aware of the
potentiality for renewal as the ageless soul experiences
the ageing of the body. In 'Sailing to Byzantium' he
writes:

That is no country for old men. The young
In one another's arms; birds in the trees,
— Those dying generations — at their song;
The salmon-falls, the mackerel-crowded seas,
Fish, flesh, or fowl, commend all summer long
Whatever is begotten, born and dies.
Caught in that sensual music, all neglect
Monuments of unageing intellect.

An aged man is but a paltry thing,
A tattered coat upon a stick, unless
Soul clap its hands and sing, and louder sing
For every tatter in its mortal dress,

Pierce thy Heart to Find the Key

Nor is there singing school but studying
Monuments of its own magnificence;
And therefore I have sailed the seas and come
To the holy city of Byzantium.

This verse might be a clarion call to us as we advance
in years, a credo for an adult education of the spirit
which knows no end. To it we may add the following
lines from T.S. Eliot's 'East Coker':

Old men ought to be explorers.
Here and there does not matter
We must be still and still moving
Into another intensity
For a further union, a deeper communion
Through the dark cold and the empty
            desolation,
The wave cry, the wind cry, the vast waters
Of the petrel and the porpoise. In my end is my
            beginning.

The goal is the flowering of the spirit. It is expressed by
a strangely magical modern poem. 'The Tree' by Karle
Wilson Baker:

My life is a tree
Yoke fellow of the earth;
    pledged

By roots too deep for remembrance
    To fill my place.
But high in the branches of my green Tree there is
    a wild bird singing:
Wind free are the wings of my bird:
She hath built no mortal nest.

The same theme is echoed in the following lines by
Juan Ramón Jiminez:

I have the feeling that my boat has struck,
    down there in the depths
    against some great thing
And nothing happens.
Nothing ... silence ... waves ... nothing.
Or, has everything happened, and are we standing
    quietly now in the new life?

We might also quote another brief poem,'Indwelling',
by T.E. Brown. In their delicate simplicity, these lines
express the whole problem of the transformation of the
soul in the New Age — the responsibility imposed on
each of us to open himself to a higher self:

If thou couldst empty all thyself of self
    Like to a shell dishabited
Then might He find thee on an ocean shelf

And say: This is not dead,
And fill thee with himself instead.

But thou art so replete with very thou
And hast such shrewd activity
That when He comes He'll say: It is enow
Unto itself. 'Twere better let it be,
It is so small and full, and has no need of Me.

Aquarius is an airy sign under which the soul aspires
to the living contact with the spiritual sun. Stephen
Spender offers us a beautiful vision of the Aquarian
Age, when the waters of the spirit are poured out:

I think continually of those who were truly great
Who from the womb remembered the soul's
                              mysteries
Down corridors of light where the hours are suns
Endless and singing. Whose lovely ambition was
That their lips, still touched with fire
Should tell of the spirit, clothed head to foot
                    with song.
                .....What is precious
Is never to forget ... never to allow
Gradually the traffic to smother
With noise and fog the flowering of the spirit.

109

Near the snows, near the sun, in the high fields
See where their names are fêted by the waving
grass...
The names of those who in their lives fought
for life,
Who wore in their hearts the fire's centre:
Born of the sun they travelled a short way
towards the sun
And left the vivid air signed with their honour.

The vision of wholeness implies that the earth is in fact a living sentient creature of which we men are an integral part. To realise our relationship to the wholeness of life we must develop, in Teilhard de Chardin's phrase, the 'Sense of Earth'. Only in this way may we come to know the spirit of earth. We find this principle expressed by Evelyn Nolt in 'The Glory Which is Earth':

Man, tread softly on the Earth
What looks like dust
Is also stuff of which galaxies are made.

The green of Earth's great trees and simple grasses
Is the same music played in red
Throughout our trunks and limbs

The first eye broadcast thought.

110

Pierce thy Heart to Find the Key

Function is the eye of dust.
Fragrance is the flower's eye.
The furred and feathered eye is freedom.
If we cannot see that dust looks back at us
If we do not see Mind in the flower's scent
If we will not see thought in the animal
It is because we bind our eyes
To stay Evolution's seeing.

> O Blessed Earth. O patient Earth
> We struggle upward to the Sun
> Forgetting what we as dust knew
> Forgetting what we as flowers saw
> Forgetting what we as animal are
> Forgetting humanness is synthesis
> Of dust, flower, animal and something more.

O Earth, living, breathing, thinking Earth
On the day we treasure you
As you have treasured us
Humanness is born.

> And throughout all Light
> A Radiance leaps from star to star
> Singing: A Son is born
>   HUMANITY

The re-emerging of the ageless wisdom and the quickening of the spirit in our time entails an expansion and acceleration of consciousness, which as pires to apprehend and blend with the whole. At the opening of our epoch, a number of great figures appeared who had achieved a species of cosmic consciousness. These figures included Walt Whitman, AE, W.B. Yeats and Edward Carpenter. All of them were cognisant of the eternal nature of the soul, and also of the fact that it requires many lives to glean the harvest of experience on earth. In the following free verse by Edward Carpenter, one can hear the voice of cosmic consciousness:

> There is no peace except where I am, saith
> the Lord,
> I alone remain, I do not change.
> As space spreads everywhere and all things
> move and change within it,
> But it moves not nor changes,
> So I am the space within the soul, of which
> the space without
> Is but the similitude or mental image;
> Comest thou to inhabit Me thou hast the
> entrance to all life —
> Death shall no longer divide thee from those
> thou lovest.

Pierce thy Heart to Find the Key

I am the sun that shines upon all creatures
    from within —
Gazest thou upon Me thou shalt be filled with
    joy eternal.
Be not deceived. Soon this outer world shall
    drop off —
Thou shalt slough it away as a man sloughs
    his mortal body.
Learn even now to spread thy wings in that
    other world,
To swim in the ocean, my child, of Me and my
    love.
Ah, have I not taught thee by the semblances
    of this outer
world, by its alienations and deaths and mortal
    sufferings — all for this,
        For Joy, ah joy unutterable.

With such development of the cosmic sense, there will
inevitably be a surge of love. We will recognise that the
same divinity which burns in ourselves burns in the
core of all other living things, and we will salute it in
them. The New Age is characterised by the emergence
of groups bound by love and a readiness for sacrificial
service to the whole. This will entail a deepening and
enrichment of personal relationships and of true
individuality. For the impulse which fires the New Age

is the working of the Avatar of Synthesis. And the
promise it holds is echoed by David Gascoyne:

Not in my life-time, the love I envisage:
Not in this century it may be. Nevertheless
    inevitable,
Having experienced a foretaste of its burning
And of its consolation, although locked in
    my aloneness
Still, although I know it cannot come to be
Except in reciprocity; I know
That true love is gratuitous and will race
    through
The veins of the reborn world's generations,
    free
And sweet, like a new kind of electricity.

The love of heroes and of men like gods
Has been for long a strange thing on the
    earth;
And monstrous to the mediocre. They
In whom such love is luminous can but
    transcend
The squalid inhibitions of those only half
    alive.
In blind content they breed who never loved
    a friend.

114

Pierce thy Heart to Find the Key

In 'A cosmic Outlook', Frederick Myers offers a
tremendous vision of the goal and the way:

On! I have guessed the end; the end is fair,
  Not with these weak limbs is thy last race run;
  Not all thy vision sets with this low sun;
Not all thy spirit swoons with this despair.
  Look how thine own soul, throned where all is well
Smiles to regard thy days disconsolate;
  Yea, since herself she wove the worldly spell
Doomed thee for lofty gain to low estate:
  Sown with thy fall a seed of glory fell;
Thy heaven is in thee and thy will thy fate.

Inward! aye deeper far than love or scorn
  Deeper than bloom of virtue, stain of sin,
  Rend thou the veil and pass alone within,
Stand naked there and feel thyself forlorn.
Nay, in what world then, Spirit, wast thou born?
  Or to what World-Soul art thou entered in;
  Feel the self fade, feel the great life begin
With Love re-rising in the cosmic morn.
  The inward ardour yearns to the inmost goal;
The endless goal is one with the endless way;
  From every gulf the tides of Being roll,
From every Zenith burns the indwelling day;
  And life in Life hath drawned thee, soul in Soul
And these are God, and thou thyself art they.

Pierce thy Heart to Find the Key

The recovery and re-emergence of the spiritual
world-view will dispel the spectre of fear of death and
bring an inner certainty of the eternal nature of the
soul. In the words of the *Bhagavad Gita:*

> Never the spirit was born; the spirit shall cease to
> be never,
> Never was time it was not; end and beginning
> are dreams.
> Birthless and deathless and changeless remaineth
> the spirit forever.
> Death hath not touched it at all, dead though the
> house of it seems.

A similar truth is expressed by Sidney Royse Lysaght:

> We have dreamed dreams beyond our
> comprehending,
> Visions too beautiful to be untrue;
> We have seen mysteries that yield no clue
> And sought our goals on ways that have no ending.
> We creatures of the earth,
> The lowly born, the mortal, the foredoomed
> To spend our fleeting moments on the spot
> Wherein tomorrow we shall be entombed
> And hideously rot —
> We have seen loveliness that shall not pass,
> We have beheld immortal destinies;

116

We have seen Heaven and Hell and joined their
        their strife;
Ay, we whose flesh shall perish as the grass
Have flung the passion of the heart that dies
Into the hope of everlasting life.

It is worth noting the power of the poem's second line.
We can all recognise the mind's capacity to apprehend
and seize an idea, knowing it to be true by virtue of its
very beauty. This may not constitute proof to the
cynical intellect, but it may be a stage in the development of latent faculties of perception which may
enable us to find a truth in new fields of understanding
that cannot be weighed or measured. As Francis
Thompson stresses in 'The Hound of Heaven', reality
must be experienced in full:

Yet ever and anon a trumpet sounds
From the hid battlements of Eternity;
Those shaken mists a space unsettle, then
Round the half-glimpsèd turrets slowly wash again.
       But not ere him who summoneth
       I first have seen...

We constantly find ourselves returning to the wonder
that, within each man, is the centre through which
contact and blending with the higher planes of
consciousness may be achieved. This is the true

communion of man, the coming-of-age of romanticism, the growing up and mature recognition of our real responsibility. For as imperishable spiritual entities, we are truly total cause of our nature and even our circumstances. This is the 'glassy essence' of which Isabella speaks in Shakespeare's *Measure for Measure:*

> Proud man
> Dressed in a little weak authority,
> Most ignorant of what he's most assured,
> His glassy essence, like an angry ape
> Plays such fantastic tricks before high heaven
> As makes the angels weep.

The same point is reiterated by Browning in 'Paracelsus':

> Truth is within ourselves; it takes no rise
> From outward things, whate'er you may believe.
> There is an inmost centre in us all
> Where truth abides in fullness; and around
> Wall upon wall, the gross flesh hems it in,
> This perfect clear perception — which is truth.
> A baffling and perverting carnal mesh
> Binds it, and makes all error: and, to KNOW
> Rather consists in opening out a way
> Whence the imprisoned splendour may escape

118

Pierce thy Heart to Find the Key

Than in effecting entry for a light
Supposed to be without.

Many poets speak in the same vein. Here, for example, is John Masefield:

Here in the self is all that man can know
Of Beauty, all the wonder, all the power
All the unearthly colour, all the glow
Here in the self that withers like a flower:
Here in the self that fades as hours pass
And droops and dies and rots and is forgotten
Sooner by ages than the mirroring glass
In which it sees its glory still unrotten.
Here in the flesh, within the flesh, behind,
Swift in the blood and throbbing on the bone,
Beauty herself, the universal mind,
Eternal April wandering alone;
The God, the Holy Ghost, the atoning Lord
Here in the flesh, the never-yet explored.

This leads us to the greatest perhaps of all themes. We may approach it first through the challenge flung down by Sidney Carter, author of 'Lord of the Dance':

Your holy hearsay
Is no evidence

119

Pierce thy Heart to Find the Key

Give me the good news
In the present tense.

What happened
Nineteen hundred years ago
May not have happened,
Who am I to know?

The living truth
Is what I long to see
I cannot lean upon
What used to be.

So shut the Bible up
And show me how
The Christ you talk about
Is living now.

A reply is offered by the Irish poet, Joseph Plunkett:

I see His blood upon the rose
And in the stars the glory of His eyes
His body gleams amid eternal snows
His tears fall from the skies.

I see His face in every flower
The thunder and the singing of the birds

120

Are but His voice, and carven by His power
   Rocks are His written words.

All pathways by His feet are worn
   His strong heart stirs the ever-beating sea
His crown of thorns is twined with every thorn
   His cross is every tree.

In virtually all his work, Gerard Manley Hopkins, the
'father of modern poetry', was profoundly aware of the
divine principle in living nature. Let us consider an
example. 'Hurrahing in Harvest':

Summer ends now; now, barbarous in beauty, the
      stooks arise
   Around; up above, what wind-walks! What
      lovely behaviour
   Of silk sack clouds! has wilder wilful-wavier
Meal drift moulded ever and melted across skies?

I walk, I lift up, I lift up heart, eyes,
   Down all that glory in the heavens to gleam our
      Saviour;
   And, eyes, heart, what looks, what lips yet gave
      you a
Rapturous love's greeting of realer or rounder
      replies?

And the azurous hung hills are his world-wielding
    shoulder
Majestic — as a stallion stalwart, very-violet-
    sweet! —
These things, these things were here and but
    the beholder
Wanting; which two when they once meet,
The heart rears wings bold and bolder
    And hurls for him, O half hurls earth for him
    off under his feet.

It is worth noting Hopkins' insistence that human initiative is essential if the bridge is to be built. We must lift the heart into the living oneness to find the divine within all matter. Wholeness — the Primal Source — has poured itself into form and therefore self-hood. As divinity and wisdom play into form, an infinite diversity of life emerges, each thing 'selfing', 'going itself'. Hopkins stresses this point in another poem:

As kingfishers catch fire, dragonflies draw flame
As tumbled over rim of roundy wells
Stones ring: like each tucked string tells,
    each hung bell's
Bow swung finds tongue to fling out broad his
    name;
Each mortal thing does one thing and the same:

Selves — goes itself; MYSELF it speaks and spells
Crying WHAT I DO IS FOR ME: FOR THIS
    I CAME.

   I say more: the just man justices;
   Keeps grace: that keeps all his goings graces;
   Acts in God's eye what in God's eye he is —
   Christ — for Christ plays in ten thousand places
   Lovely in limbs, and lovely in eyes not his
   To the Father through the features of men's faces.

In short, we must not think of the lower, limited self defined by the personality and the ego. We must think instead of a higher Self which transcends all ephemeral phenomena and issues from — indeed, is one with —the timeless. As Krishna says in the *Bhagavad Gita:*

   Wherever there is a withering of the law and an upris-
   ing of lawlessness on all sides, THEN I manifest
   Myself for the salvation of the righteous and the de-
   struction of such as do evil, for the firm establishing
   of the Law, I come to birth age after age.

We thus come to the doctrine of the Avatars which runs like a golden thread through all scriptures down the ages. When human need is greatest, and when the cry of despair goes up, the Saviour manifests. In our age, he is the Avatar of Synthesis, anticipated by the faithful in both hemispheres as the Christ, the Maitreya, the Boddhisatva, the Imam Mahdi, the Messiah. At this point, it is most appropriate to quote 'The Great Invocation', given to the world in 1945, for all who are drawn to the New Age thinking will wish to know and use it.

> From the point of Light within the Mind of God
> Let Light stream forth into the minds of men
> Let Light descend on earth.
>
> From the point of Love within the Heart of God
> Let Love stream forth into the hearts of men
> May Christ return to earth.
>
> From the centre where the Will of God is known
> Let purpose guide the little wills of men
> The purpose which the Masters know and serve.
>
> From the centre that we call the race of men
> Let the Plan of Light and Love work out
> And may it seal the door where evil dwells.
>
> LET LIGHT AND LOVE AND POWER
> RESTORE THE PLAN ON EARTH.

In 'Transfiguration', Edwin Muir expresses a similar anticipation:

> But He will come again it's said though not
> Unwanted and unsummoned; for all things,
> Beasts of the field and woods and rocks and seas
> And all mankind from end to end of the earth
> Will call him in one voice. In our own time
> Some say, or at a time when time is ripe.
> Then He will come, Christ the uncrucified,
> Christ the discrucified, his death undone,
> His agony unmade, his cross dismantled,
> Glad to be so — and the tormented wood
> Will cure its hurt and grow into a tree
> In a green springing corner of young Eden
> And Judas damned take his long journey backward
> From darkness into light and be a child
> Beside his mother's knee, and the betrayal
> Be quite undone and never more be done.

The coming of the New Age involves a passage through a time of tribulation and this is what we are now experiencing. But 'look up, for your redemption draweth nigh'. It is inevitably an apocalyptic time. We approach the apotheosis of the age of materialism and egoism. The collapse of outworn forms, the confusion in society — all may be the direct consequence of the pressure of the energies of the living spirit working for the birth of the new society based on harmony and love. And a vision of wholeness nurtures the conviction that the powers of light are indeed pouring themselves into the earth for its redemption, and that, before this century is out, we will indeed have attained a time of transformation. Such transformation will entail not only a physical reclaiming of this polluted planet but a spiritual one as well — a factor largely ignored in discussions about conservation and ecology. Again, it is Hopkins who suggests what we may hope to witness:

> The world is charged with the grandeur of God.
>   It will flame out, like shining from shook foil;
>   It gathers to a greatness, like the ooze of oil
> Crushed. Why do men then now not reck his rod?
> Generations have trod, have trod, have trod;
>   And all is seared with trade; bleared,
>   smeared with toil;
>   And wears man's smudge and shares man's
>   smell: the soil
> Is bare now, nor can foot feel, being shod.
> And for all this, nature is never spent;
>   There lives the dearest freshness deep down
>   things;
> And though the last lights off the black West went
>   Oh, morning, at the brown brink eastward,
>   springs —

Pierce thy Heart to Find the Key

Because the Holy Ghost over the bent
   World broods with warm breast and with ah!
      bright wings.

We are now entering a time of transfiguration for
man. Although the advent of the Aquarian Age is an
extended process, this last quarter of our 20th Century
will be a time of vital change, with immense hope for
man's future. But such change entails a profound
responsibility for each of us — a responsibility to think
positively, in order that the powers of light may be
effectively channelled. In *A Sleep of Prisoners*,
Christopher Fry expresses the urgency incumbent
upon us:

> The human heart can go the lengths of God.
> Dark and cold we may be, but this
> Is no winter now. The frozen misery
> Of centuries breaks, cracks, begins to move;
> The thunder is the thunder of the floes,
> The thaw, the flood, the upstart Spring.
> Thank God our time is now when wrong
> Comes up to face us everywhere,
> Never to leave us till we take
> The longest stride of soul men ever took.
> Affairs are now soul size.
> The enterprise
> Is exploration into God.

> Where are you making for? It takes
> So many thousand years to wake
> But will you wake for pity's sake?

Let us close with a similar admonition from James
Elroy Flecker:

> Awake, awake, the world is young
> For all its weary years of thought
> The starkest fights must still be fought,
> The most surprising songs be sung!

And for a final Envoi, this by F. C. Happold, which
gives a clarion call for the New Age.

> A wind has blown across the world
> And tremors shake its frame
> New things are struggling to their birth
> And naught shall be the same
> The earth is weary of its past
> Of folly, hate and fear,
> Beyond a dark and stormy sky
> The dawn of God is near.

> A wind is blowing through the Earth
> A tempest loud and strong
> The trumpets of the Christ, the King,
> Thunder the skies along
> The summons to a high crusade
> Calling the brave and true
> To find a new Jerusalem
> And build the world anew.

Index of Authors Quoted

129

Index

STILLPOINT PUBLISHING

*Books that explore the expanding frontiers
of human consciousness and invite fresh
thinking about the nature of mankind*

*For a free catalog, write to
Stillpoint Publishing
Box 640 Walpole, NH 03608
USA*